WEiRD CHRiSTMAS

JOEY GREEN

ILLUSTRATIONS BY LISA K. WEBER

BLACK DOG
& LEVENTHAL
PUBLISHERS
New York, New York

Photos on pp. 19, 87 courtesy of AP Photo; p. 59 courtesy of AP Photo/Keystone, Dorothea Mueller;
p. 65 courtesy of AP Photo/Chick Harrity; p. 92 courtesy of AP Photo/Julie Jacobson.

ISBN 1-57912-476-3

Library of Congress Cataloging-in-Publication Data on file at the offices of the publisher.

Cover and interior design by Sheila Hart Design, Inc.

Manufactured in the United States of America

Published by
Black Dog & Leventhal Publishes, Inc.
151 West 19th Street
New York, New York 10011

Distributed by
Workman Publishing Company
708 Broadway
New York, New York 10003

g f e d c b a

OTHER BOOKS BY JOEY GREEN

For Elaine

C · O · N · T · E · N · T · S

Introduction

W. C. Fields, who said he hated Christmas, died on Christmas day. So did Charlie Chaplin, the comedian who once claimed to be better known than Jesus. On Christmas Day, John Philip Sousa wrote "The Stars and Stripes Forever," the USSR detonated a nuclear bomb in the Arctic Circle, and Dick Tracy married Tess Truehart. The most popular Christmas song of all time was written by a Jew. And on Christmas Eve, even the most protective parents encourage their children to leave out cookies and milk for a fat, bearded stranger preparing to break into their home by way of the chimney.

Welcome to Weird Christmas.

On December 25, millions of people around the world celebrate Jesus' birthday-even though no one really knows on what day Jesus was actually born. But we do know that December 25 marks the birth of Sir Isaac Newton, Clara Barton, Humphrey Bogart, Anwar Sadat, and Little Richard. Christmas also marks the day on which George Washington crossed the Delaware, Hong Kong surrendered to the Japanese, and Mikhail Gorbachev resigned as head of the Soviet Union. It's the day a jury declared serial killer Ed Gein insane, protestors wielding machine guns executed former Romanian dictator Nicolae Ceausescu and his wife, and an unknown assailant murdered six-year-old JonBenet Ramsey, the reigning Little Miss Colorado. And it all began in ancient Rome, as a pagan holiday celebrating the resurrection of the Persian sun god, Mithras.

Maybe there isn't anything weird about Christmas at all. Maybe it makes perfect sense that Americans celebrate Jesus' birthday every year by chopping down 27 million fir trees. Perhaps there's nothing strange about the fact that on Christmas Eve the streets of Caracas, Venezuela, are blocked off so people can rollerskate to church. And maybe Christmas Eve was an ideal time for rock star Johnny Ace to play a friendly game of Russian Roulette and shoot himself in the head. Who am I to say "Bah, Humbug"? You be the judge.

I

WEIRD
Birthday

A Random Date,
a Quirky Star,
and No Room
at the Inn

Why December **25**?

After the winter solstice, the day of the year with the least sunlight in the Northern Hemisphere, the number of daylight hours begins to increase. For centuries before Jesus was born, pagans celebrated the "rebirth of the sun" on the winter solstice with wild festivals. Scandinavian tribes celebrated the festival of Yule (the origin of the word Yuletide) to commemorate the resurrection of the sun as the giver of light and warmth. The Romans celebrated Saturnalia (a week-long festival beginning on December 17 that was dedicated to Saturn, the god of agriculture, and to the renewed power of the sun). People decorated their homes with greenery, lit candles and bonfires, exchanged gifts, prepared special foods, and got rip-roaring drunk.

Around 60 B.C., Persians brought Mithraism—a mystery religion revolving around the sun god Mithras—to Rome. Mithraism spread throughout the empire, reaching as far as Britain. The majority of Romans were soon celebrating Natalis Solis Invicti (Latin for "birthday of the invincible sun") on December 25 in honor of Mithras. The Romans' Julian calendar, devised in 46 B.C. by astronomer Sosigenes, incorrectly declared December 25 to be the shortest day of the year (the winter solstice actually takes place around December 21). Around A.D. 274, Emperor Aurelian proclaimed Mithraism the official state religion of Rome, making the sun god the supreme god of the Roman Empire. The growing popularity of Mithraism posed a serious threat to Christianity. (Interestingly, initiates to Mithraism were baptized, promised a share in the resurrection, and took part in a regular communion meal of bread and wine.)

Initially, the Christian Church did not celebrate the birth of Jesus. At the end of the second century A.D., Christian theologian Clement of Alexandria mentioned in his writings that Egyptians of his time celebrated May 20 as Jesus' birthday, since the Gospel of Luke states that the shepherds (who were told by an angel of Jesus' birth) were watching their flocks by night, which was only done at lambing time in the spring. Around A.D. 245, Christian scholar Origen of Alexandria announced that it was a sin to celebrate Jesus' birthday "as though he were a King Pharaoh."

Sometime between A.D. 274 and 336, determined to eradicate the rival pagan celebrations of Saturnalia and Natalis Solis Invicti, the Church decided to celebrate Jesus' birth on December 25, despite the fact that no one knows the actual day on which Jesus was born. To make Christianity more acceptable to pagan converts, the Church transformed "the rebirth of the sun" to the birth of Jesus as "the light of the world" and "the sun of righteousness," instituting a day of prayer and assimilating many existing pagan practices into the Christian celebration. In 337, Roman emperor Constantine embraced Christianity, was baptized, and declared Christianity the official state religion. In 350, Pope Julius I officially declared December 25 as the birthday of Jesus. In 354, Bishop Liberius of Rome officially adopted December 25 as the day to celebrate the birth of Jesus, adding the holy day to the Roman calendar. (The Eastern Orthodox Church and the Ukrainian Catholic Church still follow the Julian calendar established by Julius Caesar in 45 B.C., and celebrate Jesus' birthday on January 6.) In A.D. 400, Pope Sixtus III conducted the first midnight Mass on Christmas at the church of Santa Maria Maggiore in Rome.

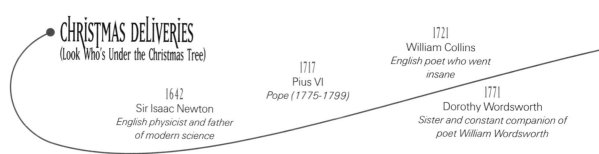

CHRISTMAS DELIVERIES
(Look Who's Under the Christmas Tree)

1642
Sir Isaac Newton
English physicist and father of modern science

1717
Pius VI
Pope (1775-1799)

1721
William Collins
English poet who went insane

1771
Dorothy Wordsworth
Sister and constant companion of poet William Wordsworth

The Strange Star of Bethlehem

Only the Gospel of Matthew tells of a star over Bethlehem. Matthew claims that the star "went forward and halted over the place where the child was. The sight of the star filled [the Wise Men] with delight." As described, the star does not act like a star at all, but seems to act more like a comet. Still, neither stars nor comets swoop down to earth and position themselves over a house. Was there really a star? Or did the author poetically invent a supernatural star to give the story more spiritual pizzazz?

POSSIBLE EXPLANATIONS

☆ Astronomers have calculated that Halley's comet, discovered by English astronomer Edmund Halley in 1682, passed by the earth in 12 B.C.

☆ In 1603, German astronomer Johannes Kepler calculated that the planets Jupiter and Saturn were in conjunction in the constellation of Pisces in May of 7 B.C., creating the appearance of a bright star in the sky. Kepler also found a reference by the rabbinical writer Isaac Abravanel (1427–1508) stating that Jewish astrologers predicted that the Messiah would arrive when Jupiter (symbolizing the king of the Roman gods) and Saturn (symbolizing justice) were in conjunction in the constellation of Pisces (symbolizing the land of Israel).

☆ The star almanac of Sippar, an ancient clay tablet

1821
Clara Barton
Nurse who founded the American Red Cross

1868
Eugenie Besserer
Actress who played Al Jolson's mother in The Jazz Singer

1876
Mohammed Ali Jinnah Karachi
Founder and governor general of Pakistan

1878
Louis Chevrolet
Founder of the Chevrolet Motor Company and designer of its first automobile

1883
Maurice Utrillo
French artist known for his paintings of Paris street scenes

found about thirty miles north of Babylon, details three conjunctions of Jupiter and Saturn in 7 B.C.

☆ In 6 B.C., Mars, Jupiter, and Saturn converged in the constellation of Pisces. In 1604, Johannes Kepler calculated that these three planets overlap every 805 years.

☆ Astronomer Michael Molnar of Rutgers University determined that on April 17, 6 B.C., the moon eclipsed Jupiter (symbolizing the Roman god) in the constellation of Aries (symbolizing Judea) in the east. Jupiter, moving from west to east across the sky, became stationary on August 21, then reversed direction, coming to a stop in Aries on December 29, then reversing direction again. (The orbits of the outer planets frequently seem to go backward when viewed from the Earth, which revolves faster around the sun.)

☆ In 5 B.C., Chinese astronomers of the Han dynasty observed a *sui-hsing* ("broom star" or comet) near the constellation Capricorn "for more than seventy days." In the Middle East, this star would appear above the eastern horizon in the spring. In 1977, three British astronomers, David Clark of the Royal Greenwich Observatory, John Parkinson of Dorking's Mullard

Who Put the X in Xmas?

Christmas is sometimes spelled Xmas, much to the consternation of some, who fear that the abbreviation is a secular attempt to rob Christmas of its spiritual meaning. It isn't, nor does the "X" represent the crucifix. Rather, Xmas derives from the Greek word for Christ: Xristos.

1887
Conrad Hilton
Founder of Hilton Hotels

1892
Dame Rebecca West
Novelist, critic, and political writer best known for her books The Thinking Reed *and* The Strange Necessity

1893
Robert L. Ripley
Cartoonist who created "Ripley's Believe It or Not"

1899
Humphrey Bogart
Academy Award-winning actor who starred in Casablanca, The Maltese Falcon, *and* The African Queen

Space Science Laboratory, and Richard Stephenson of Newcastle University theorized that this "broom star" was a nova—an exploding star. Other astronomers insist that radio and X-ray wavelengths from such a supernova would still be detectable to this day.

☆ Astronomers have calculated that the planets Venus and Jupiter were in conjunction on August 12, 3 B.C. and again on June 17, 2 B.C.

☆ Finally, some people believe that the Star of Bethlehem was actually a spaceship. An extra-terrestrial astronaut, mistaken as "God," impregnated Mary by extrasensory means to breed a more spiritually advanced civilization on Earth, then returned to Earth nine months later to witness the birth.

Sorry, No Vacancy

The Gospel of Luke tells us that Jesus was born in a stable because there was no room at the inn, but the inn wasn't necessarily a commercial lodging. In the original Greek, the word used in Luke is "kataluma," which can be translated to mean "inn," "house," or "guest room." At that time in Palestine, peasants lived in meager homes and kept their farm animals penned in the space under a raised wooden floor, to provide heat for the humble abode. It seems much more likely that Joseph and Mary showed up at a the home of one of Joseph's distant relatives in Bethlehem, found the guest room full, and stayed in the manger for a few nights before moving up to the main floor or to the guest room.

WERE THE WISE MEN REALLY WISE?

Only the Gospel of Matthew mentions the Wise Men. "Some wise men came from the east to Jerusalem," states Matthew, without specifying the number of wise men or whether any of them were kings. Having seen the star rise, the wise men journeyed to Jerusalem and asked where they could find the infant king of the Jews. If the wise men were so wise, why didn't they know exactly where to find the baby Jesus? King Herod, a brutal ruler, soon learned that the mysterious wise men were seeking the infant King of the Jews and his paranoia was aroused. The wise men were hardly wise to let a heinous tyrant know that a newborn infant was destined to usurp his power.

Herod then asked his chief priests where this "messiah" was to be born. They replied that the prophet Micah had predicted that the birth-place would be Bethlehem—which would indicate that the wise men were unfamiliar with the book of Micah (again calling their wisdom into serious question). Herod summoned the lost wise men, asked them the exact date on which the star had first appeared, and then instructed them to

1903
J. Edward Bromberg
*Actor who appeared
in the movies*
Rebecca of Sunnybrook
Farm, Mark of Zorro, *and*
Phantom of the Opera

1904
Gerhard Herzberg
*Canadian physicist who won the
1971 Nobel Prize in chemistry
for determining the electronic
structure of molecules*

1906
Clark Clifford
*U.S. Secretary of Defense
(1968–69) who persuaded
President Lyndon Johnson to
de-escalate the Vietnam War*

1907
Cab Calloway
*Jazz musician best known
for his hit song
"Minnie the Moocher"*

go find the child in Bethlehem and report back to him so he could worship the child. Did the wise men honestly believe that the ruthless Herod intended to worship the baby Jesus? The wise men followed the star, and after paying homage to the baby and giving him gifts of "gold and frankincense and myrrh," were warned in a dream not to go back to Herod. Instead, they returned to their own country by a different route. Why did the wise men need a dream to warn them that Herod might perceive the child as a possible threat to his throne? Weren't they wise enough to realize the potentially dire consequences on their own?

When Herod realized that the wise men had deceived him, he ordered his soldiers to kill all male children two years and under in Bethlehem and the surrounding area, calculating the possible age of the infant king based on the information given to him by the alleged wise men.

If the wise men were so wise, why didn't they realize that their failure to return to Herod might provoke the vicious ruler to order the deaths of innocent children and endanger the baby Jesus, forcing his family to flee to Egypt? Were the wise men really wise, or were they bumbling fools?

1908
Helen Twelvetrees
Actress who starred in the movies
The Painted Desert, Bad Company,
and State's Attorney

1909
Marguerite Churchill
Actress who appeared in the
movies The Big Trail,
Girl Without a Room, *and*
Dracula's Daughter

1909
Mike Mazurki
Professional wrestler and actor
who played a dim-witted thug in
the movies Kismet, Some Like It
Hot, *and* Farewell My Lovely

1912
Tony Martin
Singer best known for his hit
song "It's a Blue World"

Who Were the Wise Men?

Around the third century A.D., African church father Tertullian called the Wise Men *fere regis* (Latin for "almost kings"). About that same time, Christian scholar Origen first suggested that there were three Wise Men, perhaps based on the fact that Matthew mentions three gifts—gold, frankincense, and myrrh. Many people jump to the conclusion that the Wise Men were royalty because the gifts were valuable. The obscure collection *Excerpta Latina Barberi*, written in the sixth century A.D., names the three visitors Gaspar, Melchior, and Balthasar. A medieval Irish description depicts the three visitors as representatives of three major races. Christian literature describes them as astrologers or Zoroastrian priests who journeyed from either Persia, Babylon, the Arabian desert, or the land once ruled by the queen of Sheba. The alleged remains of the three magi—St. Gaspar, St. Melchior, and St. Balthasar—are housed at the Kölner Dom, the great cathedral in Cologne, Germany.

1915
Nora Dunfee
Actress who starred in the movies Forrest Gump *and* Lorenzo's Oil

1918
Anwar El-Sadat
Egyptian president (1970–81) who signed a historic peace treaty with Israel

1924
Rod Serling
Creator of the television series The Twilight Zone

1928
Dick Miller
Actor who starred as Walter Paisley in Roger Corman's cult classic horror movie A Bucket of Blood *and appeared in* The Dirty Dozen, Rock 'n' Roll High School, The Terminator, After Hours, *and* Pulp Fiction

1929
Billy Horton
Member of the rock group the Silhouettes, best known for their hit song "Get a Job"

1929
Chris Kenner
Rhythm-and-blues musician who wrote the hit song "I Like It Like That"

The Manger Mystery

While most Christmas nativity scenes depict the Wise Men visiting Jesus in the manger, the Gospel of Matthew (the only Gospel to mention the Wise Men) says that the Wise Men visited Jesus in a "house"—not a manger—in Bethlehem.

Declaration of Independence

In a letter to John Adams dated April 11, 1823, former U.S. president Thomas Jefferson wrote: "The day will come when the mystical generation of Jesus by the Supreme Being as his father, in the womb of a virgin, will be classed with the fable of the generation of Minerva in the brain of Jupiter."

1931
Carlos Castaneda
Author of the mystic novel Separate Tales of Reality

1932
Little Richard
Musician best known for his hit songs "Good Golly Miss Molly," "Tutti-Frutti," "Long Tall Sally," and "Lucille"

The Word

December 25 was first called "Christmas" in the ninth century. The word is derived from the Old English Cristes Maess—meaning Mass of Christ (the word christos is Greek for "messiah"). Christmas is called Noël in French, Navidad in Spanish, and Natale in Italian—all derived from the Latin Natalis (as in Natalis Solis Invicti, the Latin name of the original pagan holiday).

1933
Mabel King
Actress who played Mama on the television sitcom What's Happening!

1936
Ismail Merchant
Producer of the films Room with a View *and* Howard's End *(with director James Ivory)*

1937
O'Kelly Isley
Member of the Isley Brothers whose hit songs include "Shout," "Twist and Shout," and "It's Your Thing"

1943
Hanna Schygulla
Actress who starred in numerous plays and movies directed by Rainer Werner Fassbinder and appeared in the films The Delta Force *and* Dead Again

1943
Ravish Malhotra
Indian cosmonaut and back-up crew member for Soyuz T-11

THE NIGHT BEFORE CHRISTMAS

Christmas Eve is the only Christian holiday celebrated like a Jewish holiday. All Jewish holidays start at sundown and last until the following sundown.

And One to Grow On

Strangely, few people celebrate Christmas by placing more than 2,000 lit candles on a cake and singing "Happy Birthday" to Jesus.

1944
Rick Berman
Producer of the television series Star Trek: The Next Generation, Deep Space Nine, *and* Voyager

1945
Ken Stabler
Oakland Raiders quarterback

1945
Noel Redding
Leader of the Noel Redding Band and bass guitarist in The Jimi Hendrix Experience

1944
Henry Vestine
Member of the rock group Canned Heat, best known for the hit songs "Goin' Up the Country" and "On the Road Again"

1945
Gary Sandy
Actor who played Andy Travis on the television sitcom WKRP in Cincinnati

December Down Under

In the Southern Hemisphere, December 25 falls near the summer solstice, the longest day of the year. Yet, people living in the land down under celebrate Christmas with customs devised around the shortest day of the year. If Christmas truly is a celebration of "the light of the world" returning to banish times of darkness, shouldn't people in the Southern Hemisphere celebrate it at their own winter solstice—June 21?

1946
Jimmy Buffett
Musician best known for his hit songs "Margaritaville," "Come Monday," and "Changes in Latitudes-Changes in Attitudes"

1948
Barbara Mandrell
Country singer and co-host of the television variety series The Mandrell Sisters, *best known for the hit song "If Loving You Is Wrong"*

1949
Sissy Spacek
Actress who starred in the movies Carrie, The Shining, *and* Coal Miner's Daughter

1946
Larry Csonka
Miami Dolphins running back

1949
Dan Pastorini
Los Angeles Raiders quarterback

Getting Close at Christmas

The earth is closest to the sun (91.4 million miles) around January 1 and farthest from the sun (94.5 million miles) in July. The seasons are caused by the tilt of the earth's axis (23.5 degrees), not by the earth's distance from the sun. The tilt provides the Northern Hemisphere with its most direct sunlight (and longer daylight hours) between March and September, while the Southern Hemisphere receives the most direct sunlight during the other half of the year. And of course, the more direct sunlight there is, the hotter the temperature gets. That's why, when it is summer above the equator, it is winter below.

JINGLE BELLS

Mr. Layne Hall of Silver Creek, New York, was born on Christmas Day in 1884. When he died 105 years later, on November 20, 1990, Hall had a valid driver's license, making him the world's oldest legal driver.

1954
Robin Campbell
Member of the rock group UB40

1957
Shane MacGowan
Lead singer of the Irish rock group the Pogues

1954
Annie Lennox
Singer for the Eurythmics, best known for her hit songs "Sweet Dreams Are Made of This" and "Here Comes the Rain Again"

1957
Jillie Mack
Actress who appeared on the television series Magnum P.I. *and married its star, Tom Selleck*

1958
Ricky Henderson
Baseball's "Stolen Base King" who played for the New York Yankees and Oakland A's

What Are the Twelve Days of Christmas?

In A.D. 567, the Council of Tours proclaimed that the twelve days of Christmas span from Christmas Day on December 25 to Epiphany on January 6. The Catholic and Protestant Churches celebrate Epiphany as the day the Wise Men visited the baby Jesus with their gifts. In Eastern Churches, Epiphany celebrates the baptism of Jesus. In truth, the New Testament does not mention on what date the Wise Men visited the baby Jesus or precisely when Jesus was baptized. The Council of Tours may have established the Twelve Days of Christmas as a political compromise to embrace the Eastern Orthodox Church and the Ukranian Catholic Church, which both celebrate the birth of Jesus on January 6. At one time, people gave gifts throughout the twelve days of Christmas, rather than all at once on Christmas morning.

Happy Circumcision

In the Christmas song, "The Twelve Days of Christmas," the gift given on the eighth day, marking Jesus' circumcision, is "eight maids a-milking." A more appropriate gift might have been the present given on the tenth day— "ten lords a-leaping."

1959
Missy Cleveland
Playboy Playmate for April 1979

1959
Michael P. Anderson
African-American astronaut who was a crew member aboard two missions of the Space Shuttle Endeavor

1960
Amy Grant
Country singer best known for her hit song "That's What Love Is"

1960
Marisa Acocella Marchetto
New Yorker *cartoonist and creator of the comic strip* She

THE CIRCUMCISION CRAZE

If Jesus was born on December 25, and if he was circumcised in accordance with Jewish law on the eighth day after his birth (as stated in the Gospel of Luke), Jesus was circumcised on what is today celebrated as New Year's Day. Circumcision (January 1) is one of the six holy feast days celebrated by the Roman Catholic Church, despite the fact that the Catholic Church does not require males to be circumcised.

1962
Mary Ellen Clark
Olympic bronze medalist for diving

1969
Bernhard Jr.
Prince of the Netherlands

1971
Noel Hogan
Member of the rock group the Cranberries

1976
Yazmin Fiallos
Miss Universe 1996 and Miss Honduras (1996)

When was Jesus born?
(A Solve-It-Yourself Mystery)

Although the birth of Jesus is celebrated on December 25, no one knows exactly when Jesus was born. Can you figure out the real date of Jesus' birthday?

The Gospel of Luke states that the shepherds who were told by an angel of Jesus' birth were "keeping watch over their flocks at night." This was done only in the spring, at lambing time.

Emperor Caesar Augustus conducted censuses of Roman citizens in 28 B.C., 8 B.C., and A.D. 14. Roman historian Flavius Josephus mentions in his book *Antiquities* that a census was taken in Judea in A.D. 6.

The only record of the birth of Jesus is in the New Testament, and only two of the four Gospels (Matthew and Luke) mention it. Neither Matthew nor Luke mention on what day of the week, month, or year Jesus was born.

The Gospel of Luke states that Jesus was born at a time when Roman Emperor Caesar Augustus ordered a census, while Quirinius was governor of Syria.

The Gospels of both Matthew and Luke claim that Jesus was born while Herod reigned as the king of Judea. Herod ruled from 37 B.C. until his death in 4 B.C.

Quirinius was not the governor of Syria during the reign of Herod. Quirinius governed Syria sometime between 4 and 1 B.C.

During Jesus' lifetime, the Romans used the Julian calendar. The Julian calendar numbered the years starting with the year in which Rome was allegedly founded—1 A.U.C. (*Anno urbis conditae*—Latin for "the year of the establishment of the city"). In 1278 A.U.C. (more than 500 years after the birth of Jesus), a Roman monk, Dionysus Exiguus, renumbered the years beginning with the year of Jesus' birth, rather than from the founding of Rome. Unfortunately, he miscalculated the year of Jesus' birth to be 753 A.U.C.—four to eight years after the actual date—and this is the year that became A.D. 1.

The Gospel of Luke says that Jesus started to teach when he was "about thirty years old," in "the fifteenth year of Tiberius Caesar's reign," which was 782 A.U.C. (or A.D. 28).

In the Gospel of John, Jesus is told "You are not yet fifty."

Caesar Augustus ruled between 44 B.C. and A.D. 14.

Pontius Pilate ruled as governor of Judea from A.D. 26 to 36, according to Roman historian Flavius Josephus.

These are the only clues we have to determine when Jesus was actually born. If you can determine the actual date from the above information, you will be revered as a genius or despised as a heretic.

Other Famous Virgin Births

As early as 3000 B.C., ancient Egyptians worshipped the god Osiris, who fathered through the virgin Isis an earthly son named Horus. The birth was announced by three wise men, symbolized by three stars in Orion's Belt pointing to Osiris' star in the east, and took place in a manger on the winter solstice. Historians recognize ancient Egyptian statues of the virgin mother Isis suckling her baby Horus as the precursor to depictions of Madonna and Child.

Around 2000 B.C., Persians began worshiping Mithra, a sun-god born to a god father and a human virgin mother named Anahita (referred to as "The Immaculate Virgin Mother of Lord Mithra") in a cave on December 25. The birth was witnessed by shepherds who brought gifts.

During the second millennium B.C., ancient Greeks worshipped the god Dionysus, who was the son of the god Zeus and the Theban virgin princess Semele. According to Greek mythology, Dionysus was born on the winter solstice.

Around 2000 B.C., ancient Syrians and Babylonians worshipped the god Dumuzi, who was born on the winter solstice to a virgin named Mylitta.

As early as 1400 B.C., Hindus in India began worshipping the divine son Krishna, born to the human virgin Devaki and the god Vishnu on the winter solstice. According to Hindu scripture, Krishna's birth in a cave was heralded by a star.

Around 1400 B.C., Attis, a deity worshipped in Phrygia and later throughout the Roman Empire, was said to be the son of the virgin Nama and to have been born on the winter solstice.

The Egyptian Pharaoh Amenhotep III, of the seventeenth dynasty (1382–1344 B.C.), was hailed as the son of the virgin Queen Mutemua.

Buddha, a mortal sage named Siddhartha Gautama (563–483 B.C.), was said to have been born of a virgin named Maya and was visited by wise men who acknowledged his divinity.

According to the play Amphitruo, written by Roman playwright Titus Maccius Plautus (circa 254–184 B.C.), the great Greek hero Hercules was born to the god Zeus and the virgin Alcmena.

In the first century A.D., Roman historian Livy wrote a history of Rome in which he explained that Mars, the Roman god of war, fathered twins Romulus and Remus through a human vestal virgin mother named Silvia.

As early as the tenth century A.D., the Aztecs of ancient Mexico worshiped Quetzalcoatl, a great Toltec deity, who was a son of the virgin goddess Coatlicue.

ON CHRISTMAS DAY

(Weird Events That Took Place on Christmas)

498

Frankish king Clovis I, the first Germanic king to become an orthodox Christian, baptized himself—before proceeding to kill the other kings who had previously been his allies.

800

In a surprise move, Pope Leo III placed a crown on the head of Charlemagne at St. Peter's Basilica in Rome and pronounced him emperor of all Christian lands—an act which led to the birth of the Holy Roman Empire. Charlemagne had merely been expecting Pope Leo III to consecrate his son the king of the Franks and the Lombards.

875

Charles the Bald was crowned emperor of Rome. He was followed by Charles the Fat, who was succeeded by Charles the Simple.

1024

King Boleslaw I of Poland, determined to consolidate his power over the lands he had conquered since first being crowned king by Emperor Otto III in 1000, had himself crowned king of Poland a second time by the archbishop of Gniezno.

1046

Pope Clemens VI crowned German king Henry III emperor of the Holy Roman Empire. Three years later, Henry III appointed his cousin, Count Bruno van Egisheim, Pope Leo IX.

1066

William the Conqueror, the illegitimate son of the Duke of Normandy (better known as Robert the Devil), was crowned king of England.

1522

Turkish troops occupied the island of Rhodes in the Aegean Sea, initiating the rapid decline of what was once a wealthy, independent state of Greece and the home to many artists, poets, and philosophers.

1643

Captain William Mynors of the British East India Company named an island approximately 224 miles south of the Indonesian Island of Java in the Indian Ocean "Christmas Island." First sighted in 1615 by Richard Rowe, the island is a source of phosphate (a chemical with no Yuletide significance).

1688

English king James II fled to France. A Roman Catholic whose favoritism toward Catholics angered many of his English subjects, James had been overthrown after his wife gave birth to a son, inciting his opponents who feared the prospect of another Catholic ruler.

Columbus's Crash Course

On Christmas Eve 1492, one of Columbus's three ships, the *Santa Maria*, crashed into a coral reef off the shore of Hispaniola, the island shared today by Haiti and the Dominican Republic. On Christmas Day, a group of Taíno Indians, led by their chief, Guacanagari, paddled out to help the conquistadors aboard the sinking *Santa Maria* salvage their usable cargo. Columbus ordered his men to use the frames and planking of the *Santa Maria* to build a fort (15 kilometers east of what is now Cap-Haïtien, Haiti), which he named La Villa de Navidada (the village of the Nativity). Columbus left forty men at the fort and returned to Spain. He returned a year later to discover that the fort had been razed to the ground and his men massacred by Arawak Indians.

1741

Swedish astronomer Anders Celsius introduced the centigrade scale for measuring temperature. On the centigrade scale, 0 degrees is the freezing point of water and 100 degrees is its boiling point. Between those two fixed points the scale is divided into 100 equal parts (centigrades). On the Fahrenheit scale, invented by German physicist Gabriel Daniel Fahrenheit in 1714, 32 degrees is the freezing point of water and 212 degrees is its boiling point. In 1948, the ninth General Conference on Weights and Measures officially renamed the centigrade scale the Celsius scale to honor its inventor. Most countries in the world use the Celsius scale. The United States uses the Fahrenheit scale.

1745

Prussia and Austria signed the Treaty of Dresden, giving most of Silesia to the Prussians. Austria had seized Silesia in 1526. Prussia had invaded Silesia in 1742. Today Silesia is shared by Poland and the Czech Republic.

1758

Johann Georg Palitzch spotted a comet whose return had been predicted by English astronomer Edmond Halley. Halley had observed a comet in 1682, calculated its orbit, and proved that the comets seen by astronomers in 1531 and 1607 were one and the same. Before Halley, people believed that comets appeared haphazardly, but Halley proved that comets orbited the sun. He predicted that the comet seen in 1531, 1607, and 1682 would return in 1758. The comet became known as Halley's Comet. It appears on an average of every 77 years. Some people believe that the Star of Bethlehem was actually Halley's Comet, but astronomers have shown that Halley's Comet would have appeared in 9 B.C.

1777

British explorer James Cook became the first European explorer to reach what he called Christmas Island, in the Pacific Ocean. The largest island formed by coral in the world, Christmas Island lies 1,334 miles south of Honolulu, Hawaii. The British used the island as a nuclear test site from 1957 until 1962, when the United States conducted nuclear tests there—a strange way of sharing the Christmas spirit. In 1979, radioactive Christmas Island became a part of the independent island nation of Kiribati.

1814

On Christmas Eve, the United States and the United Kingdom signed the Treaty of Ghent in Belgium, ending the War of 1812. News traveled slowly to America, and British commander general Sir Edward Pakenham, unaware that the war had ended, sent more than eight thousand troops to capture New Orleans. On January 8, 1815, fifteen days after the war had ended, General Andrew Jackson led his troops to victory against the British in the Battle of New Orleans, also known as "The Needless Battle."

A GEORGE WASHINGTON CHRISTMAS

In 1776, having lost Long Island and Manhattan to the British, General George Washington began leading 2,400 troops across the icy Delaware River at about eleven at night on a rainy, freezing-cold Christmas in the hope of making a surprise attack on a Hessian (German) force celebrating the holiday at their winter quarters in Trenton, New Jersey. The next morning, Washington's force, separated into two columns, marched to the outskirts of Trenton and attacked the 1,400 unsuspecting Hessian troops, capturing nearly one thousand Hessians and losing only four American lives.

Lacking adequate artillery and manpower, Washington was forced to withdraw from Trenton—but news of the victory raised American morale, reviving hope that victory for the patriots was possible and inspiring many soldiers to reenlist.

In his famous 1897 painting of Washington crossing the Delaware, artist Emanuel Leutze depicts a U.S. flag that was not adopted by Congress until six months after Washington crossed the Delaware, He also portrays the Durham boats Washington and his troops used as being approximately twenty feet long when they were actually more than twice that length, and shows the crossing taking place during the day (although it actually happened at night).

1818

On Christmas Eve, Joseph Mohr, priest at the Church of
St. Nikolaus in Oberndorff, Austria, wrote the words to
"Silent Night." His church organist, Franz Joseph Gruber, composed the music that
same night, and the carol was sung at midnight Mass for the first time.

1837

At the Battle of Okeechobee in Florida, U.S. troops defeated the Seminole Indians.

1847

The Christmas carol "O, Holy Night," written by French composer Adolphe Adam,
was sung for the first time at midnight Mass.

1862

Taking a much-needed break from the Civil War, 40,000 people watched men from
the Union army play baseball at Hilton Head, South Carolina.

1868

In his last important act as president, Andrew Johnson granted an unconditional
pardon to all Southerners who had participated in the Civil War—despite the fact
that Amendment 14 to the Constitution, passed five months earlier, had given
Congress the sole authority to grant amnesty.

1896

John Philip Sousa wrote the melody to a song that had haunted him for days and
titled it "The Stars and Stripes Forever."

1908

Boxer Jack Johnson knocked out Tommy Burns and became the first black heavyweight champion.

1917

The play *Why Marry?* by Jesse Lynch Williams opened at the Astor Theater in New York and later became the first drama to win a Pulitzer Prize.

1922

Ernest Hemingway's first wife, Hadley, decided to join her husband for Christmas in Switzerland, where he was working as a news correspondent. As a surprise, she brought a suitcase packed with all of the existing copies of his untitled first novel and several unpublished short stories. At the Paris railroad station, the suitcase was stolen.

1925

U.S. admiral Latimer disarmed Nicaraguan rebels in support of President Adolfo Diaz's regime.

Peace on Earth, . . . Nah, on Second Thought . . .

Just after midnight on Christmas day in 1914, five months after the outbreak of World War I, the majority of German troops on the front lines ceased fire and began singing Christmas carols. At various points along the Eastern and Western fronts, Russian, French, and British soldiers heard German brass bands accompanying the joyous singing. At dawn, German soldiers emerged from their trenches and slowly crossed "no-man's-land" to the Allied lines, calling out "Merry Christmas" in Russian, French, and English. The Allied soldiers, at first suspicious, soon emerged from their trenches to shake hands with the Germans, exchange gifts of cigarettes and plum puddings, and sing Christmas carols. At one point, opposing British and German troops played a good-natured game of soccer. The unofficial Christmas Truce lasted a few days—until the soldiers were ordered to return to the previously scheduled war.

1926

Hirohito became emperor of Japan, succeeding his father, Emperor Yoshihito.

1932

During English King George V's Christmas dinner speech, his chair collapsed.

1939

Lionel Barrymore read the Charles Dickens classic, *A Christmas Carol,* on *The Campbell Playhouse* on CBS radio, starting an annual tradition.

1940

Pal Joey, the musical by Richard Rodgers and Lorenz Hart, premiered in New York City.

1941

Hong Kong surrendered to Japan, which went on to occupy the British colony until 1945. Having neutralized the U.S. Pacific fleet with the bombing of Pearl Harbor on December 7, the Japanese invaded Malaya, Hong Kong, and the northern Philippines on December 10. Hong Kong's population had grown to 1.6 million after the Japanese invaded China in 1937, but with the Japanese occupation of Hong Kong, nearly 1 million Chinese returned to China.

1944

British prime minister Winston Churchill went to Athens, Greece, to seek an end to the civil war that had erupted there earlier that month. British troops helped drive Greek communists out of Athens, restoring the monarchy to Greece.

1946

The Chinese National Government, meeting in Nanking and led by Chiang Kai-shek, adopted its Constitution, pledging universal suffrage. When the Chinese Communists, led by Mao Tse-tung, conquered mainland China in 1949, the Chinese National Government fled to the island of Taiwan. Only citizens of Taiwan adhere to the Constitution.

1950

Dick Tracy married Tess Truehart in the comic pages. The couple later became parents of a baby girl named Bonnie Braids.

1958

Eighteen-year-old Richard Starkey received his first drum set. He soon adopted the stage name Ringo Starr.

1959

Sony unveiled the world's first transistor television.

1962

The USSR detonated a nuclear bomb in a test at Novaya Zemlya, a pair of islands inhabited by reindeer in the Arctic Ocean —an usual way to promote religious tolerance and peace on earth.

Happy Xmas (War Is Over)

In December 1969, Beatle John Lennon and his new wife, Yoko Ono, proclaimed their peace campaign with the slogan "War Is Over! If You Want It" (signed "Happy Christmas from John & Yoko") in full-page advertisements in the world's major newspapers and on prominent billboards in New York, Los Angeles, Montreal, Toronto, London, Paris, Amsterdam, Rome, and Athens.

In 1971, John and Yoko released the single song, "Happy Xmas (War Is Over)," recorded with the Harlem Community Choir. The song became the first single by a Beatle that failed to make America's Hot 100. The song did not gain widespread popularity until after John Lennon's death in 1980.

As a Beatle, Lennon infuriated the Christian Right in America when he said that the Beatles were more popular than Jesus (prompting radio stations in the Bible Belt to urge listeners to burn Beatles albums) and again with the Beatles' song "The Ballad of John and Yoko," in which he seems to compare himself to Jesus, expressing a fear of his own crucifixion.

O, Little Town of Vietnam

For Christmas in 1972, the United States ceased Operation Linebacker II, an intensive bombing campaign against North Vietnam, for 36 hours. The full-scale air raid, which began on December 18 by order of President Richard Nixon when North Vietnamese negotiators walked out of secret peace talks in Paris and refused to return, lasted for a total of eleven days. During that time, 700 B-52 sorties and more than 1,000 fighter-bomber sorties dropped an estimated 20,000 tons of bombs on North Vietnam—half the total tonnage of bombs dropped on England during World War II.

1964
Female Beatle fans attacked George Harrison's girlfriend Patti Boyd.

1967
Beatle Paul McCartney and actress Jane Asher announced their engagement at a McCartney family party. By July, the engagement was off.

1968
Apollo 8 went into orbit around the moon on Christmas Eve and astronaut Frank Borman read the opening passages from the Biblical Book of Genesis.

1969
Five Israeli gunboats escaped from Cherbourg harbor in France.

1969
In Tokyo, Seiko introduced the first quartz wristwatch. The Quartz 35 SQ Astron sold for $1,250.

Oh What Fun It Is to Ride in

1971

The longest pro football game in sports history finally ended when Garo Yepremian kicked a field goal in the second quarter of sudden-death overtime. The Miami Dolphins defeated Kansas City, 27-24. The total game time was 82 minutes and 40 seconds.

1973

Astronauts aboard Skylab made a seven-hour space walk to photograph Comet Kohoutek.

1974

To promote toy safety at Christmas time, the Consumer Products Safety Commission printed up 80,000 buttons that read: "For Kids' Sakes, Think Toy Safety." The buttons—made with sharp edges, lead-based paint, and pins that came off easily and could be swallowed by a child—were immediately recalled.

An Electric Car On Christmas Day in 1985, David Turner and Tim Pickhard completed the longest battery-powered drive in history, traveling on a single charge from Land's End, England (the southernmost point in Great Britain), to John o' Groat's, Scotland (the northernmost point in Great Britain), in a battery-powered Freight Rover Leyland Sherpa driven by a Lucas electric motor. The trip took four days and, without batteries, would have required an 875-mile-long extension cord.

ALL I WANT
FOR CHRISTMAS
ARE SOME LEVI'S
501 JEANS

On Christmas Day in 1991, Mikhail S. Gorbachev, the eleventh leader of the Soviet Union, appeared on national television to announce his resignation as president of a Communist superpower that no longer existed. As he spoke, the Soviet hammer-and-sickle flag was lowered over the Kremlin in Moscow, and the traditional white, blue, and red Russian flag was raised in its place. Just four days earlier, representatives from eleven of the former Soviet republics had met in the Kazakh capital of Alma Ata, where they formally established the Commonwealth of Independent States, disbanding the Soviet Union and abolishing Gorbachev's job as president.

1977
Israeli prime minister Menachem Begin met with Egyptian president Anwar Sadat in Egypt.

1979
The USSR invaded Afghanistan to stop a civil war and protect Soviet interests.

1984
The sphere of chemical gasses released from a West German satellite created the first man-made comet visible in the sky. The yellowish-green "comet" appeared in the constellation Virgo.

1989
Japanese scientists achieved −271.8 degrees Celsius, the coldest temperature ever recorded.

1989
On Christmas Eve, Manuel Noriega, accompanied by two bodyguards, drove to a Dairy Queen ice-cream store in Paitilla, a commercial neighborhood of Panama City, dialed the number for the Vatican's local diplomatic mission, spoke to Monsignor Laboa, and requested sanctuary. Laboa sent a nunciature vehicle to pick up Noriega at the Dairy Queen.

1989
Dissident playwright Václav Havel was elected president of Czechoslovakia.

1992
French climber Christine Janin reached the summit of Mount Aconcagua in South America, becoming the first woman to climb the highest peak on every continent.

1997
To welcome Pope John Paul II to Cuba, the communist government allowed its citizens to celebrate Christmas as a holiday. The Castro regime had ended the celebration of Christmas in 1969.

1998
Seven days into their journey, British mogul Richard Branson, American millionaire Steve Fossett, and Per Lindstrand, of Sweden, abandoned their attempt to make the first nonstop around-the-world balloon flight, giving up near the coast of Hawaii.

2004
French climber Alain Robert, a self-proclaimed "Spiderman," climbed to the top of the world's tallest building, the 1,679-foot Taipei 101, in Taipei, Taiwan. Having previously scaled New York's Empire State Building in 1994 and the Petronas Twin Towers in Kuala Lumpur, Malaysia, in 1997, Spiderman took four hours to make his Christmas Day climb—twice as long as he expected—due to wind and rain.

WEIRD Santa

2

Santa

will work for milk & cookies

Who on Earth
Is Santa Claus?

The mythical notion of Santa Claus evolved from the real-life Saint Nicholas, a gaunt-looking bishop born in the late third century to wealthy Christian parents in the ancient Lycian seaport city of Patara in Asia Minor (present-day Turkey). Nicholas became bishop of the coastal town of Myra (now called Demre). A tall, slender man with a long, white beard, Nicholas wore a traditional red-and-white bishop's robe and a miter (a tall hat with peaks in front and back), and carried a staff with a crook at one end.

Legend holds that while aboard a ship to Palestine, Nicholas calmed a violent sea with his prayers—making him the patron saint of sailors. Another legend tells that Nicholas prayed over the dead bodies of three young brothers who had been murdered by an evil innkeeper, chopped up, and hidden in a tub of brine. His prayers purportedly brought the three youngsters back to life, making Nicholas the patron saint and protector of young children. Yet another tale maintains that when an impoverished father was about to sell his three young daughters into lives of prostitution because he had no money for their dowries, Nicholas anonymously threw three bags of gold through the window of the girls' home so they could marry whomever they wished. He was then dubbed the patron saint of unwed women.

When Roman emperor Gaius Diocletianus persecuted the Christians, the Romans imprisoned Nicholas. The slender bishop was released under the rule of Emperor Constantine (who later converted to Christianity) and attended the first Council of Nicaea in A.D. 325.

Nicholas is believed to have died on December 6, 342. He was buried in his church at Myra. Over the centuries that followed, Christians dedicated more than 2,000 churches to St. Nicholas and made him the patron saint of Russia, Greece, and Sicily. In 1087, Italian sailors or merchants stole his alleged remains and took them to Bari, Italy. These relics were enshrined in the eleventh-century basilica of San Nicola, where they remain to this day.

In the Netherlands, the three bags of gold that Saint Nicholas reportedly gave to the poor girls became a bulging sack of presents that "Sinter Klaas" (a Dutch variant on the name Saint Nicholas) handed out to children on December 6 (the Feast Day of St. Nicholas). Legend holds that Sinter Klaas traveled by donkey, and his gifts were usually fruits, nuts, candies, and figurines.

During the Protestant Reformation of the sixteenth century, the commemoration of Saint Nicholas was banished in Europe, prompting Christians to create Father Christmas in England, Père Noël in France, and Weihnachtsmann in Germany. The Dutch kept the Saint Nicholas tradition alive. Children filled their wooden shoes with straw for Saint Nicholas's donkey, placed them in front of the fireplace on the traditional night of the Saint's arrival, and in return received edible treats. In the seventeenth century, Dutch settlers brought this custom to New Amsterdam (now New York City) in the American colonies, where the shoes were replaced by stockings and the English-speaking population turned the Dutch name for Saint Nicholas—Sinter Klaas—into "Santa Claus." Americans fused the legend with northern European tales of a winter spirit who gave gifts to good children and punished bad ones.

In 1809, American author Washington Irving (best known for his short story "The Legend of Sleepy Hollow") published *A History of New York* under the pseudonym Diedrich Knickerbocker. In the book, Irving described Saint Nicholas as a plump, jolly man who wore a broad-brimmed hat and huge breeches, smoked a long pipe, rode over treetops in a horse-drawn wagon, and filled children's stockings with presents.

In 1822, Dr. Clement C. Moore, a professor at the General Theological Seminary in New York, wrote a poem entitled "A Visit from St. Nicholas" to entertain his family on Christmas Eve. A friend mailed a copy to the *Troy Sentinel*, which printed the anonymous poem on December 23, 1823.

Other publications soon reprinted the poem, popularizing some of Moore's key additions to Santa Claus folklore: the suit of fur, the chimney through which he enters homes, the bundle of toys, and the sleigh pulled by eight flying reindeer. Moore, who publicly admitted authorship in 1838, described Santa as "a jolly old elf" and named the reindeer Dasher, Dancer, Prancer, Vixen, Comet, Cupid, Donder, and Blitzen. Moore seems to have melded Sinter Klaas with the Finnish legend of "Old Man Winter," who rides a sleigh pulled by reindeer down from the mountains to deliver snow.

From 1863 and 1886, the popular magazine *Harper's Weekly* ran a series of engravings by political cartoonist Thomas Nast, who built upon Moore's image of Santa Claus, depicting him as an overweight yet jolly old man who reads letters from children, checks

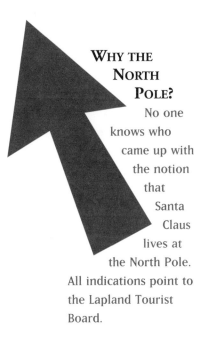

WHY THE NORTH POLE?
No one knows who came up with the notion that Santa Claus lives at the North Pole. All indications point to the Lapland Tourist Board.

his list, builds toys in his workshop at the North Pole, rides a sleigh pulled by reindeer, and places toys in stockings hung over a fireplace.

Department store Santas began appearing in the late 1800s—consulting with eager children about their holiday wishes .

In 1897, Francis P. Church, editor of the *New York Sun*, wrote an editorial in response to a letter from an eight-year-old girl, Virginia O'Hanlon, who asked whether there really was a Santa Claus. "Yes, Virginia, there is a Santa Claus," replied the unsigned editorial. "He exists as certainly as love and generosity and devotion exist, and you know that they abound and give to your life its highest beauty and joy. Alas! How dreary would be the world if there were no Santa Claus! It would be as dreary as if there were no Virginias." The response became one of the most famous editorials ever written and was reprinted annually until 1949, when the *New York Sun* went out of business.

In 1931, the Coca-Cola Company commissioned Swedish painter Haddon Sundblom to depict Santa Claus for its advertisements. Sundblom produced a new painting of Santa Claus every year until 1964, giving the jolly man a red coat and hat trimmed with white fur, a thick black belt, and replacing the long-stemmed pipe with a bottle of Coca-Cola.

The Real Miracle of Christmas

Santa Claus is an overweight senior citizen who never ages, oversees a highly productive workshop that supplies the world with toys, spryly leaps down chimneys, gobbles up cookies, and seems strangely immune to heart attacks, strokes, Alzheimer's disease, arthritis, and diabetes.

Rollo the Red-Nosed Reindeer?

In 1939, Santas at Montgomery Ward department stores across the United States gave away 2.4 million copies of a souvenir booklet entitled "Rudolph the Red-Nosed Reindeer," featuring a whimsical poem written by Chicago advertising copy-writer Robert May and illustrated by his friend, artist Denver Gillen. May single-handedly invented the story and initially named the reindeer Rollo, but Montgomery Ward executives nixed the name. May then proposed the name Reginald, which they also rejected. The group ultimately settled upon Rudolph, a name preferred by May's four-year-old daughter.

In 1947, songwriter Johnny Marks, a friend of May's, set the poem to music. In 1949, "singing cowboy" Gene Autry recorded the song, which promptly rocketed to the top of the Hit Parade, becoming the second-best-selling song of all time, after Bing Crosby's recording of another holiday favorite, Irving Berlin's "White Christmas."

Oh, Just Call Them "Thunder and Lightning"

Donner and Blitzen, two of the reindeer named in the popular Christmas song "Rudolph the Red-Nosed Reindeer," were originally named Dunder and Blixem in the anonymous poem "A Visit from Saint Nicholas," first published on December 23, 1823, in the *Troy Sentinel*. The original names, Americanized spellings of the Dutch words Donder and Blicksem, mean "thunder" and "lightning."

In 1837, publisher Charles Fenno Hoffman printed a version of "A Visit from Saint Nicholas" with several alterations. "Blixem" was changed to "Blixen" (to rhyme with "Vixen") and "Dunder" was changed to "Donder" (perhaps to better align the spelling with the pronunciation). In 1844, the poem's real author, Clement Clarke Moore, a Bible professor at New York's General Theological Seminary, reprinted "A Visit from Saint Nicholas" in a volume of his own poetry and changed his original "Dunder and Blixem" to "Donder and Blitzen." The word *blitzen* is German for lightning. In 1906, *The New York Times* published Donder's name as Donner, although the change may have occurred earlier in another publication. *Donner* is the German word for "thunder."

The popularity of the 1949 song "Rudolph, the Red-Nosed Reindeer," sung by Gene Autry, etched the names Donner and Blitzen into Americans' collective consciousness.

REINDEER GAMES

While both male and female reindeer have antlers, males lose theirs during the Christmas season due to hormonal changes, and do not grow new ones until the spring. Male reindeer retain their antlers during the Christmas season only if they have been castrated. This means that Santa's reindeer, always depicted with antlers, are either females or castrated males.

Have Yourself a Merry Little Christmas

According to the folk medicine of the Lapps, an ethnic group living in northern Scandinavia, powdered reindeer antlers can increase virility. They export the potency powder to the Japanese.

Fast Forward

In the town of North Pole, Alaska (population 1,735), located thirteen miles east of Fairbanks, you can visit Santa Claus at his house, tour Santa's workshop, and camp at the Santaland RV Park. Cities and towns that don't have the resources to deal with letters to Santa Claus often forward them to North Pole, Alaska. "Fairbanks postmaster Raymond Clark says the town gets about 80,000 Santa letters a year," reported *Fortune Magazine* in 2001. "A full-time and a part-time employee deal with the flood and pass many letters along to volunteers and civic groups. But they manage to answer only about 7 percent. 'It's been a constant problem,' Clark says."

HOLIDAY SPIRIT

While some people speculate that Rudolph the Red-Nosed Reindeer gets his glowing proboscis from imbibing alcohol, Norwegian scientist Odd Halvorsen of the University of Oslo hypothesized in a 1986 issue of the journal *Parasitology Today* that Rudolph's red nose might be the result of a parasitic infection in his respiratory system.

Dutch Treat

The first Dutch settlers to sail to America had a figure of Saint Nicholas mounted on the front of their ship.

Attack
of the Cheap-Suit Santas

In 1994, the Cacophony Society—a loose coalition of dedicated pranksters founded in 1986-decided to mock the consumerism of the holiday season by dressing up in cheap Santa suits, getting drunk, and marauding around downtown San Francisco for a night of revelry. The "Cheap-Suit Santas" barhopped, raided department stores and the lobbies of luxury hotels, sang naughty Christmas carols, and chanted "Ho, ho, ho!" and "You better watch out!" Every December since then, irreverent and rowdy Santas have been taking to the streets in major cities, creating merry mayhem in a night of Kringle chaos billed variously as Santacons, Santarchy, Santa Rampages, Santasms, and Santafadas.

The idea for the nationwide Santa invasions began with San Francisco's Michael Michel, a leader of the Cacophony Society who circulated the group's newsletter around the Bay area and once posted hundreds of fake fliers around the city that announced: "Lost python 15 feet long. Do not attempt to catch alone!!! Reward $300." In 1990, determined to expand the Cacophony Society to other cities, Michel printed up fliers for the "Brotherhood of Magnetic Light" and handed them out at a UFO convention in Los Angeles. The flier announced that Jesus was scheduled to land in a spaceship on a local beach at

EQUAL OPPORTUNITY SANTA?

Every year, Santa Claus bypasses millions of Buddhist, Hindu, Muslim, Jewish, and other non-Christian homes worldwide. Yet, Santa Claus has never been slapped with a class-action lawsuit for discrimination. Could this be yet another miracle of Christmas?

How Many Santa Clauses Are There?

After the Civil War, Santa Claus began appearing in department stores, the commercial cathedrals of consumerism. As of 1999, there were 44,426 malls and shopping centers across the United States. That means there were as many as 44,426 Santa Clauses in the United States alone.

9:13 the following night. Dressed in a silver-and-gold lamé jumpsuit, Michel waited on the beach to see what would happen. A young man wearing a priest's robe and calling himself "Reverend Al" walked up the coastline, followed by dozens of others. That night Michel and Reverend Al recognized each other as kindred spirits and began planning more elaborate events that Reverend Al, the group's self-proclaimed Grand Instigator, announced via the Internet or newsletters.

The 1995 San Francisco Santacon attracted some fifty drunken Santas who stormed the Hyatt Regency Hotel, invaded the Emporium shopping center, romped through a Christmas carnival, purloined some holiday decorations, hung one of the Cheap-Suit Santas from a stoplight post, mooned tourists from a cable car, and went barhopping all over the city. San Francisco police pulled over a city bus full of Santas, forced them into a line-up, and arrested some suspects.

In 1996, the annual Santacon moved to Portland, Oregon, where the evening climaxed with a stand-off at a local mall between a line of police in riot gear and some 100 renegade Santas singing Christmas carols.

In 1997, more than 300 Santas from San Francisco boarded a

Northwest Airlines flight to Los Angeles. The next day, more than 400 drunk Santa Clauses—some riding skateboards and scooters, some pushing one another around in shopping carts, and some spraying one another with party confetti—gathered in the parking lot of CBS studios in Los Angeles and boarded three chartered school buses. They marched over the sand dunes of Venice Beach to wade in the ocean, visited Muscle Beach (where a weightlifter bench-pressed one of the Santas 100 times), converged on Mann's Chinese Theatre, stopped traffic on Hollywood Boulevard, raided the Scientology Winter Wonderland site, went to a strip joint on Sunset Boulevard, and visited the Griffith Park Observatory to reenact the knife fight scene from the James Dean movie *Rebel Without a Cause* (renamed Rebels with a Claus). Along the way, they smoked pot, lit fireworks, and pulled one another's pants down. They posed for photos with tourists and handed out demented gifts—rusty batteries, beheaded Barbie and Elmo dolls, and cigarettes ("Here's a little coal for your lungs!").

By 1998, Santa Rampages had spread to New York City, where some ninety Santas protested at the United Nations with signs reading "U.N. Out of North Pole," "No More Reindeer Games," and "Hands Off My Pole." They then converged on the tree at Rockefeller Center, invaded the Plaza Hotel, romped through Central Park, and occupied Tavern on the Green.

Ever since then the Santa infestations have taken on an even larger life of their own, spreading to cities around the world including Anchorage, Ann Arbor, Auckland, Austin, Baltimore, Bangkok, Barcelona, Bellingham, Boston, Chicago, Cymru (Wales), Dallas, Denver, Detroit, Eugene, Ft. Lauderdale, Helsinki, London, Los Angeles, Madison, Montreal, New Orleans, New York City, Oklahoma City, Ottawa, Portland, Reno,

Global Warning

The needle of a compass does not point to the North Pole, at the northern tip of the earth's axis. A compass needle points to the magnetic north pole (created by the earth's magnetism), which moves over time. As of 2005, the magnetic north pole was located at 82.7 degrees north latitude by 114.4 degrees west longitude—northwest of Ellef Ringnes Island in Canada.

Sacramento, San Francisco, Seattle, St. Johns (Newfoundland), Tijuana, Tokyo, Toronto, Tuscaloosa, Vancouver, Wellington, and Winnipeg.

The naughty Santas, determined to reclaim Christmas from Hallmark and desanitize the holiday season, lambaste the sacred notion of Santa Claus as a harmless and jovial old man who encourages mass consumerism. Instead, participants embrace the mischievous side of the bearded old man, simultaneously proclaiming their freedom and individuality. The invasions have attracted Santas wearing Darth Vader masks, Santas with purple hair, female Santas, multiracial Santas, Santas wearing gas masks, pimp Santas, miniskirted Santa vixens, Santas wearing kilts, Mrs. Clauses wearing red, fur-lined lingerie, and demonic elves. Along the streets, Santas press their bearded faces against the windows of fancy restaurants, shake hands with bewildered people, and ask passersby whether they've been naughty or nice. They sing lewd carols, stop traffic, frighten children, amuse adults, give inappropriate gifts (ketchup packets, slices of processed cheese, and small computer parts), use aerosol snow to spray graffiti, and plaster stickers reading "naughty" or "nice" on startled tourists. They shout twisted Christmas phrases at random: "Come sit on my knee, little girl," "How would you like Santa to come down your chimney?" "Hell, no! We won't ho!" "And what would you like for Christmas?" "Don't be such a ho!" "Does your turkey need stuffing?" "What part of 'ho' don't you understand?" "Wanna see the North Pole?"and "You had me at 'ho.'" And they chant "Naughty! Naughty Naughty!"

Hundreds of drunken Santas in Los Angeles have gone ice skating and plastered the trees outside City Hall with wrapping paper, garlands, and ornaments. In Chicago, hoards of bearded Santas have bicycled through the city streets. In New York, Santas have climbed the Brooklyn Bridge, staged a protest in the park demanding "More Milk and Cookies," and marched through Macy's chanting "Charge it!" Santas have gone bowling in Vancouver, go-carting in New Orleans, and ridden bumper cars in London. But mainly the Santas tend to overtake famous landmarks, hit numerous bars, and visit strip joints and sex toy shops.

The seemingly sacrilegious Santas have actually revived a long tradition of rambunctious Santas. The docile Santa Claus popularized by the poem "The Night Before Christmas," Coca-Cola ads, and Hollywood movies bears little resemblance to the unruly, mischievous Santa Claus of the nineteenth century, who played practical jokes and perpetrated devious pranks. In Pennsylvania Dutch country, people would dress up as a masked, tattered version of St. Nicholas called Belsnickle (German for "Furred Nicholas") and visit the homes of friends and family singing drunken Christmas carols and carrying a whip or switch to chastise children who misbehaved.

He's Diabolical!
The letters in the word "Santa" can be rearranged to spell "Satan."

The first person to reach the North Pole was U.S. Naval officer Robert Peary on April 6, 1909. He never reported finding Santa's workshop, or even a giant candy cane marking the spot.

Is Anyone Home?

Black Santa

The first African-American Santa appeared in a magazine ad for Royal Baking Powder in 1910. While many African-American community groups and churches have long provided a black Santa Claus for children to visit, few shopping malls offer kids the opportunity to sit on the knees of a black Santa Claus. At the height of the Civil Rights movement in the 1960s, the Southern Christian Leadership Conference boycotted Federated Department Stores, persuading the company to hire a black Santa in Cincinnati. Today, many companies sell African-American Santa Claus figurines, but live black Santa Clauses remain a rarity at shopping malls.

Crucified Santa

In 1997, New York's Art Students League displayed in its window Robert Cenedella's painting of a crucified Santa Claus, prompting intense criticism from religious groups. The artist insisted that his painting merely satirizes how people have wrongly allowed Santa Claus to replace Jesus as the focus of Christmas. Ironically, the many commercially available ornaments that mingle the image of Santa Claus with the image of Jesus never seem to cause any public outrage. A perennial favorite is an ornament depicting Old St. Nick kneeling before the manger.

Return to Santa

Every year some 4 million letters addressed to "Santa Claus" pour into the small town of Santa Claus, Indiana (population 1,648), to be returned to sender with the "Santa Claus" postmark. Residents purportedly named the town on Christmas Eve in 1852. In 1946, industrialist Louis J. Koch built the world's first theme park in the town of Santa Claus. Originally named Santa Claus Land, the park experienced tremendous growth and is known today as Holiday World & Splashin' Safari. Other Christmas-themed businesses and street names in the town include Christmas Lake Village, Kringle Place, Santa's Lodge, Holiday Foods, and Ho Ho Ho Video.

THE REAL MIRACLE ON 34TH STREET

In the heartwarming 1947 movie *Miracle on 34th Street*, a man working as Santa Claus at Macy's department store claims to be the real Santa Claus. The Academy-Award winning film was produced by William Perlberg, a Jew.

Santarctica

In Antarctica on Christmas Day in 2003, forty Santas cooked and served Christmas dinner for more than 1,000 inhabitants of McMurdo Station, the American base on Ross Island. Santas made coffee, carved tenderloin, washed dishes, and swept floors.

The idea originated with dining attendant Allison Barden, a native of San Francisco who had witnessed the annual Santa shenanigans in her home town and decided to organize "Santarctica: The Biggest Congregation of Santas Furthest from the North Pole." In November, Barden instructed two friends who had participated in the annual San Francisco event, to mail forty Santa costumes to her in Antarctica. When a postal worker asked why they were shipping forty Santa suits to Antarctica, one of the duo replied, "Well, it would be ridiculous to ship them to the North Pole, now wouldn't it? It's not like the real Santa doesn't already have plenty."

In 2004, the forty Santas reappeared in Antarctica on Christmas Eve to parade around McMurdo Station, invade a bar to play poker, darts, and shuffleboard, and prance into a Christmas party held for all the residents of the base.

Kiwi Christmas

On December 18, 2004, at 6:45 p.m., police in Auckland, New Zealand, broke up a group of thirty heavily intoxicated men and women dressed in Santa Claus suits, fighting in a parking garage. The police, convinced that the Santas had been drinking since morning, arrested only two of the Santas for disorderly behavior.

Sick Nick

In 1998, a 72-year-old man named Ronald McDonald who volunteered as Santa Claus at the Lake Forest Park Towne Centre shopping mall in Seattle, Washington, and frequently baby-sat for neighbors' children was sentenced to twenty-six years in prison for raping a six-year-old girl at his home. With his white hair and round features, the clean-shaven McDonald closely resembled Santa Claus when he donned a fake white beard. A relative reported McDonald to the police after coming to believe that McDonald had molested the six-year-old. During a meeting with a police officer, McDonald confessed to a long history of sexual contact with at least seven other children over a period of some twenty-six years.

Good Tidings

Every year before Christmas, Santa Claus hits the beach at Fort Lauderdale, Florida, to hand out candy canes.

Santa Congress

Every year, more than one hundred authorized Santas from all over the world gather at the World Santa Claus Congress held at Bakken, the world's oldest amusement park, just north of Copenhagen, Denmark.

The congress started in 1963, when one of the performers at Bakken had a Christmas party in the middle of the summer. The Santas—from as far away as Russia, Greenland, Germany, Canada, Great Britatin, Ireland, Norway, Italy, Japan, Holland, and Venezuela—convene to discuss their work conditions, parade up and down Strøget (Copenhagen's oldest, longest and most famous pedestrian street), go to the beach for their annual beach paddle, participate in Olympic Christmas Winter Games, gather for morning exercises, dance around a Christmas tree, visit the Little Mermaid statue honoring the fairy tale by Hans Christian Andersen, tour the children's wing at the central hospital in Copenhagen, enjoy a traditional Danish Christmas dinner (with roast pork and crackling, red cabbage, caramelized potatoes, and rice pudding) at restaurant Ølgod, and select a "Santa of the Year."

Santa Champ

During the Santa Claus World Championships, held in Samnaun, Switzerland, teams of Santa Clauses from around the world compete against one another in donkey trekking, chimney climbing, snowball fighting, sledge racing, and Santa skiing—in the hope of capturing the title "Santa Claus World Champion." The annual competition began in 2000 and attracts more than 100 Santa Clauses.

You Better Watch Out

Santa Claus just may be a more devious menace than the "Big Brother" envisioned by George Orwell in his novel *1984*. Santa constantly conducts surveillance of millions of children and violates their right to privacy, determined to discern whether they are being "bad or good"—casting an even wider net than the Thought Police in Orwell's novel. The fact that Santa watches children worldwide, while they are sleeping as well as when they are awake, suggests the machinations of a voyeuristic pedophile. He also displays a deep-seated, obsessive-compulsive neurosis: he incessantly makes lists of children who are naughty and nice, then checks them not once, but twice. This behavior reflects the workings of what can only be described as a very disturbed mind.

Consider the evidence. The unkempt, long-haired, unshaven Bohemian, dressed in red (to display his communist ideology, perhaps?) enslaves helpless elves in his isolated sweatshop and relegates his wife to the role of a second-class citizen, refusing to allow her even the dignity of a first name. He goes on an annual rampage, breaking into and entering private homes by way of the chimney, stealing cookies, apples, and milk, then leaving behind toys in a feeble attempt to redistribute wealth and spread his warped Marxist-Leninist-totalitarian-tyranny.

Santa Claus apparently "drinks so heavily that his flying sleigh must be guided by a reindeer named Rudolph who—judging by his red nose—is even more drunk than Santa," noted columnist William Burril in the *Toronto Star*. "The fact that Santa Claus manages to visit every house in the world in one single night also strongly suggests a heavy personal use of hard drugs such as speed, cocaine and 'E'."

SANTA CLAUS IS WATCHING YOU

Santa's Military Escorts

In 2002, the North American Aerospace Defense Command (NORAD) announced that the Canadian Air Force had selected three Canadian fighter pilots as the official escort pilots for Santa Claus when he visited Canada during his annual Christmas Eve trip around the world. Once alerted by Canadian Air Defence Sector Operations Centre that Santa was en route, Major James Manning and Captain Daniel Bélanger would pilot two CF-18 Hornet fighters to meet him as he entered Canadian air space off the Newfoundland coast and take pictures of his sleigh. As Santa finished his trip across Canada, Captain Desmond Brophy would pilot a CF-18 Hornet fighter jet to escort Santa out of Canadian airspace to continue his Yuletide trip.

Santa Olympics

At the annual Santa Winter Olympics held every November in Gaellivare, Sweden, some fifty Santas from across Europe compete in disciplines such as shimmying up chimneys, wrapping Christmas gifts quickly and properly, riding kick-sledges, and driving reindeer. Santas from as far away as Britain, Russia, and Spain travel 745 miles to the town north of Stockholm and nearly sixty miles north of the Arctic Circle to take part in the three-day event, organized by the local folklore society in cooperation with a hotel. The top three Santas receive gold, silver, and bronze medals in the shape of miniature peaked shoes, and all participants receive consolation medals—in keeping with the Christmas spirit. To qualify for participation in the Santa Olympics, candidates must believe in Santa, share Santa's kindly spirit, be recommended by another Santa Claus, and pass a yearlong trial period.

HERE COMES SANTA CLAUS

In 1934, a store in Colorado Springs ran an advertisement urging children to call Santa on a special hotline, but misprinted the telephone number. Instead of reaching Santa Claus, children telephoned the U.S. Continental Air Defense Command. The director of operations, Colonel Harry Shoup, played along, adding a picture of Santa and his reindeer to the tracking map of North America. The North American Aerospace Defense Command (NORAD) has continued the tradition ever since.

In 1996, NORAD's Cheyenne Mountain Command Center received more than 15,000 Santa calls, and in 1997 began posting Santa tracking information on the Internet. (Normally, NORAD monitors North American aerospace for potential intruders and global aerospace for ballistic missile launches and objects orbiting Earth.)

Based on historical data, NORAD anticipates visual identification of Santa in North American airspace on Christmas Eve beginning at approximately 10 p.m. Eastern Standard Time. NORAD's tracking team issues hourly reports from 4 p.m. to 1 a.m., Mountain Standard Time, on Christmas Eve. Children and parents can receive a personal Santa update by dialing (719) 474-3980 on Christmas Eve, or by visiting NORAD on the Internet at http://www.norad.com.

In 2000, the "NORAD Tracks Santa" site received over 200 million hits during the period of December 23–27, setting a world record. Visitors to the Web site can view information about Santa collected over the years by NORAD experts, including how Santa manages to visit so many homes in one night and how NORAD's satellites detect Rudolph's red nose.

Ten Little Santas

On December 20, 1994, ten sidewalk Santas handing out fliers to promote the Great American Backrub Shop on Third Avenue in New York City gathered around a bicyclist who was hit by a van, administering first aid and directing traffic around the scene. The stunned bicyclist, 63-year-old Philip Anderson, reportedly turned to one of the Santas and asked, "Am I in the North Pole?"

Scary Santa

Every year, the *Chicago Tribune* holds a "Scared of Santa" contest, asking readers to send in photos of children shrieking with terror while sitting on Santa's lap. The three photos judged to be the best garner prizes, and the newspaper prints the winning entries and some runners-up.

Santa's Safe-Sex Helpers

In 2003 on the weekend before Christmas, young women in skimpy Santa outfits distributed 50,000 free condoms to adults (and candy to children) along Singapore's Orchard Road shopping district. The makers of Playsafe condoms sponsored the event to educate the public on AIDS prevention and to encourage safe sex.

YIPPIE!
IT'S SANTA!

On December 4, 1968, Yippie leader Jerry Rubin showed

up during a hearing of the House Un-American Activities

Committee in Washington, D.C., dressed in a Santa Claus suit and

toting a toy gun. Rubin said the toy gun was for "self-defense" and

claimed his costume was typical for the committee, which he described as "a

total circus." Rubin was barred from the hearing.

Resulting newspaper headlines announced:

"HUAC Bars Santa Claus."

You Have the Right to Remain Santa

On December 16, 2004, a Greenpeace activist dressed as Santa Claus and carrying a placard tried to enter Argentina's Congress in Buenos Aires to protest during a legislative debate over whether to let Australia ship nuclear waste to Argentina. The demonstrator's sign read: "No to nuclear waste, yes to the Constitution." The protest took place as representatives from 189 countries met in Buenos Aires for a United Nations conference on global warming.

Santa to the Finnish

Santa Claus does not live at the North Pole, say the Finns, but in Finland, near the city of Rovaniemi, the capital of Lapland, in a mountain called Korvatunturi. The proof? At Christmastime hundreds of tourists from all over the world fly to visit Santa, Mrs. Santa, the elves, and Santa's reindeer at his Santa Claus Village in Lapland.

According to the Finns, the genuine Santa Claus has always lived at Korvatunturi in Finnish Lapland and only Santa Claus, his elves, and his reindeer know the road to Korvatunturi. Santa's elves eavesdrop on children to determine whether they are bad or good and write down their observations in huge notebooks. Just before Christmas, Santa Claus reads through the notebooks and carefully chooses appropriate gifts for all the good children. In Finland, Santa personally delivers gifts to children while they are awake, but in other countries he delivers the gifts to the children's homes while the youngsters are asleep.

Although Santa Claus lives with his elves at Korvatunturi, he built his own village six miles north of the town of Rovaniemi, at the point where the northbound highway crosses the Arctic

Circle, placing his village close to an international airport and comfortable hotels for the convenience of tourists. The International Aviation Association has named Rovaniemi Airport "Santa's official airport."

At Santa Claus Village, Santa has his own greeting center, his own official Post Office, and a small collection of the big notebooks from Korvatunturi in which the elves have recorded the behavior of the world's children. Nearby Santa Park, a magical grotto, gives visitors a glimpse into how Santa Claus lives at Kovatunturi. Guests can visit Santa Claus year round at his village and can arrange to have Santa send personalized letters to children of all ages anywhere in the world.

THE SANITY CLAUS

In the 1935 Marx Brother's movie *A Night at the Opera*, Groucho and Chico discuss the clauses in a contract:

Chico: Hey, wait, wait. What does this say here? This thing here.

Groucho: Oh, that? Oh, that's the usual clause. That's in every contract. That just says, uh, it says, uh, "If any of the parties participating in this contract is shown not to be in their right mind, the entire agreement is automatically nullified."

Chico: Well, I don't know . . .

Groucho: It's all right, that's . . . that's in every contract. That's . . . that's what they call a sanity clause.

Chico: Ha ha ha ha ha! You can't fool me! There ain't no Sanity Clause!

Santa's Strip Show

On December 23, 1999, a Santa Claus at Westfield Shoppingtown Promenade Mall in Woodland Hills, California, called a mother an "evil person," angrily ripped off his beard and costume in front of the waiting children, and was escorted out by security guards.

What prompted the Santa to go ballistic?

The mother had wanted Santa to hold her crying baby for a traditional Christmas photo. When Santa refused, the pushy mom told Santa that if he put his arm around the 19-month-old boy, the baby would stop crying.

"I will not imprison your child," said Santa, who then accused the mother of torturing her baby for a photograph and dubbed her "an evil person."

The mother told Santa she planned to file a complaint against him stating that he did not belong around children. Infuriated, the Santa leapt from his throne, pulled off his beard, threw off his wig, and ripped off his coat and belt—stunning the long line of parents and children, and prompting some parents to cover their children's eyes. The exposed Santa left his red suit on the floor and disappeared into a nearby shop. Security guards quickly apprehended him and escorted him away.

GRANDFATHER FROST
and
SNOW GIRL
(Strange Santas from Around the World)

UKRAINE
Grandfather Frost and Snow Girl deliver gifts on New Year's Eve. The duo came into being after the Russian Revolution, when the Communist Party outlawed Santa Claus and Christmas celebrations.

SCANDINAVIA
Santa Claus sends a lively elf to deliver gifts to the children after the traditional Christmas Eve dinner. In Denmark and Norway, the elf is called Julenissen. In Sweden, he's called Jultomten.

JAPAN
"Santa Kurohsu" has eyes in the back of his head so he can see what children are doing.

NETHERLANDS
Saint Nicholas arrives on December 6 on a boat from Spain and rides through the streets on a white horse accompanied by his servant, Black Peter, who carries a birch rod to whip naughty children.

ITALY

La Befana, a kindly old witch who refused to join the wise men to visit the baby Jesus because she had too much housework to do, wanders throughout Italy on the eve of Epiphany (January 6) to search all the houses for the Christ Child, leaving presents for good children along the way and a lump of coal for bad ones. This is her annual attempt to make amends for not having joined the Magi.

FRANCE

Père Noël (Father Christmas) places gifts in the sabots (traditional wooden shoes) left in front of the fireplace by children. In one area of France, Aunt Airie, a caped fairy, travels with a donkey and also distributes gifts.

CHINA

Santa Claus is known as Dun Che Lao Ren ("Christmas Old Man").

GERMANY

Saint Nicholas's assistant, Knecht Ruprecht (Servant Rupert) brings candy and sweets to children on December 6, gives switches to the parents of bad children, and collects children's wish lists of the gifts they would like to receive from the Christkindl (Christ child). The Christkindl in turn sends Weihnachtsmann (Holy Night Man), who delivers the presents on Christmas Eve. From the name Christkindl evolved the character Kris Kringle, an angel-like figure who brings gifts at Christmas.

RUSSIA

Babushka, an old witch who gave the magi wrong directions on their trip to Bethlehem, attempts to atone for her sin by giving presents to all good children on the eve of Epiphany (January 6). Babushka was outlawed after the Communist Revolution.

SPAIN

The Wise Men—not Santa Claus or Father Christmas—bring Christmas gifts to children on January 6 (the day the Magi visited the baby Jesus). Children leave barley in their shoes to feed the Wise Men's camels.

Worlds' Largest Santa Gathering

On December, 19, 2004, more than five thousand people dressed as Santa Claus marched in the northern Portuguese city of Porto in an attempt to break the world record of Santa Clauses marching together. The Portuguese Santas broke the world record established in 2003 in Newtown, Wales, where 3,200 adults dressed as Santa Claus ran in the annual 4.5-mile Santa Run. The Welsh runners broke the world record previously set on December 7, 2002, when 2,685 costumed Santas paraded down the streets of Bralanda, Sweden. All participants wore red Santa costumes with matching hats, fake white beards, and black belts.

Helicopter Santa

Every year St. Nicholas arrives by helicopter in Rio de Janeiro's Marcana stadium, the biggest soccer arena in the world, as the guest of honor at a huge party with festive speeches and numerous entertainers.

The High Cost of Shaving

In December 2002, the Stoneridge Mall in Pleasanton, California, fired Tom Galletti, who played Santa Claus for sixteen years, because he lacked an authentic beard. The mall replaced him with a Santa with a real beard. Galletti's dismissal was not an isolated occurrence. Hundreds of malls across the nation now require their Santa Clauses to have natural, full, white beards. This doesn't stop precocious children from tugging on Santa's white beard to see if it's real (which could probably get downright painful during a long shift), but a genuine beard doesn't come off and risk traumatizing believing children.

Santas with authentic beards earn more money than clean-shaven Santas who don fake beards. According to the International Council of Shopping Centers, Santas with genuine beards earn an average of $8,000 a year. A Santa with a real beard, a soothing voice, and a jovial demeanor can earn up to $35,000. Santas earn an average of $35 to $50 an hour at the mall, and between $150 and $200 an hour for private parties. A high-quality Santa suit costs approximately $1,500.

Santa Claus College

There's no grueling Santa Aptitude Test, no rigorous admission requirements, and no strict grade point average to maintain. But anyone wishing to obtain a Bachelor of Santa Claus can easily enroll at any one of several prominent Santa Schools.

One of the oldest institutes of higher learning for Santas—the Harvard of Santa Universities—is the Charles W. Howard Santa School in Midland, Michigan.

Howard, a Macy's department store Santa who rode in the Thanksgiving Day Parade and served as a consultant on the 1947 classic Christmas movie *Miracle on 34th Street*, began teaching Santa Claus School in his barn in Albion, New York, in 1937. When Howard retired in 1966, one of his faithful students, Tom Valent, took over as dean and moved the school to his hometown in Michigan.

Valent, an executive vice president of a construction firm who studied at Howard's school for fourteen years and plays Santa locally, charges $300 in tuition for the intensive three-day course in "Santadom." Seminars include the history of St. Nicholas and Santa, beard-and-hair care, Santa Hygiene 101, Santa etiquette and decorum, singing, storytelling, Santa dancing, and how to "ho, ho, ho" (not too loudly, or you risk scaring small children). The Santas take field trips to learn how to drive reindeer, conduct media interviews and radio call-in shows, and familiarize themselves with the latest toys at Toys 'R' Us.

At the Midland Community Santa House, decorated with seven-foot-tall nutcrackers and animatronic elves playing piano, Valent teaches fifty students from across North America to change gloves frequently, refrain from flirting or telling off-color jokes, and how to place a child on Santa's knees (keeping Santa's hands visible at all times to avoid the appearance of impropriety). The Santas memorize all the reindeers' names and what year Rudolph was born (1939), and feed Comet and Cupid, Valent's pet reindeer. Valent also coaches the Santas on how to work with babies, children in the hospital, and children with special needs. Most important, students learn that being Santa is a privilege, not a job.

THE RIDDLE OF SANTA CLAUS

Question:

What are the three stages of man?

Answer:

1) He believes in Santa Claus.

2) He doesn't believe in Santa Claus.

3) He is Santa Claus.

Finally, the Santas suit up, sit on the throne, and hold a dress rehearsal with actual children. Upon receiving their official red Santa hat at a closing banquet, the Santas pledge to uphold Santa principles and to carry the spirit of Christmas in their hearts—because, as the graduates have learned, wearing the red outfit and white beard doesn't automatically turn you into Santa Claus. Being Santa Claus is a state of a mind.

The second most popular Santa School in North America is in Calgary, Alberta. Former real estate agent Victor Nevada, now a full-time professional Santa Claus and the author of the 329-page Santa manual titled *All About Being Santa*, is the headmaster of Santa School.

The comprehensive two-day course, held in October and limited to twenty students at $400 a head, takes place in the convention rooms of a local hotel. Instructors include an acting coach, lawyer, make-up artist, hairdresser, costumer, and professional photographer.

Nevada himself prefers to play the part of Santa Claus with a slight edge rather than portraying the milquetoast caricature promoted by Disney. With an actor's dedication, he develops his character, scripts responses to typical questions (like "Are you the real Santa?" and "Is there a bathroom in your sleigh?"), rehearses, and prefers playing to adult crowds where he can use racier material from his stand-up routine called "The Secret Life of Santa."

Nevada's Santa School curriculum covers such topics as the history of Santa Claus, his genetic origins, costuming, make-up, maintenance of wigs and beards, business fundamentals, common mistakes and how to avoid them, character development, crowd control, and how to pose properly for photographs. Students tour a toy store, and each graduating student receives a class photo and a BSC—Bachelor of Santa Claus.

The top three Santa photo companies in the United States also provide classes for their hired Santas. SantaPlus of St. Peter, Missouri, teaches prospective Santas the reindeers' names, details of Santa's life, appropriate behavior and conversation, and how to put children at ease.

Cherry Hill Photo Enterprises of Cherry Hill, New Jersey, runs Santa Claus University, providing a two-hour crash course to teach students the dos and don'ts of being a mall Santa. Students learn that Santa never gets mad, shows up drunk, picks his nose, or flirts with mothers or children (because Mrs. Claus is very important in his life). Students also learn that Santa Claus always stays jolly with a twinkle in his eye, never has a cell phone ringing in his pocket, and understands that some kids have a mom and dad while others have two moms, two dads, a single parent, or just grandparents. So Santa just calls the grown-ups "folks."

Noerr Program Corporation sends its hired Santas to Susen Mesco of American Events and Promotions in Denver, Colorado, who runs an intensive weekend course every fall that includes child psychology, sign language, makeup, acting, and descriptions of the latest toys and technology. Mesco, who has been teaching Santas since 1982, insists that Santa keep up with the times. He's got e-mail, a computer, and he recycles.

Reindeer Games

On Christmas Eve, Santa Claus may ride a sleigh pulled by eight reindeer over North America, but during the night, he frequently switches modes of transportation. Santa rides a kangaroo in Australia, he paddles a canoe in Hawaii, he rides a horse in the Netherlands, he travels by a donkey in Switzerland, and he is dropped from heaven on a golden cord into the Czech Republic.

OPERATION SANTA CLAUS

Every year, thousands of children write letters to Santa Claus. Those letters end up in the dead-letter office.

In the early 1920s, postal clerks at the New York General Post Office began reading the letters to Santa Claus (before or after their work shifts) and responding by sending gifts to children from underprivileged homes. Thanks to the classic 1947 movie *Miracle on 34th Street*, which is on television every year during the holiday season and shows the New York Post Office delivering thousands of children's letters to a department-store Santa, the number of letters addressed to Santa Claus increased from 5,000 in 1980 to more than 150,000 in 1997.

When the number of letters grew out of control, the postal clerks sought help from the public by establishing Operation Santa Claus. Now, every December at the Operation Santa Claus office at the New York General Post Office in Manhattan, New Yorkers stop by to read through heartbreaking letters that needy children have sent to Santa Claus. They choose one or more letters, and then send or personally deliver one or more gifts. Some participants who deliver the gifts personally don Santa gear for the occasion.

Inspired by New York's Operation Santa Claus, postal workers in other cities have established their own local versions of the program. Of course, it's important to screen the letters carefully. While most come from disadvantaged children, there are always a few letters from wealthy suburban kids looking for a little extra swag.

The Ten Santa Commandments

In 1932, Hampton S. Sisler, general manager of a Chicago department store called Donovan and Shields, wrote up the following ten indispensable rules of Good Santahood after he discovered an inebriated store Santa and another one complaining to children and parents about having to work long hours without a break.

Bodily hygiene is to be scrupulous. Special attention should be paid to the cleanliness of undergarments and socks.

Ditto oral hygiene. Please ask Santas to refrain from eating strong-smelling foods such as garlic. Chewing tobacco is to be discouraged.

Fingernails are to be kept short and clean. Outgrowths of nasal hair will not be tolerated.

Santas must ensure that tunics, boots, beards, and wigs are to be kept clean. An over-night laundry service will be provided.

Please ensure that correctly fitting uniforms are issued and that all tears, lost buttons, etc., are promptly repaired.

Under no circumstances may intoxicating beverages be consumed on the premises or prior to Santas taking up their duties. The penalty shall be immediate dismissal.

Santas may not congregate in uniform by the Staff entrance when off-duty or smoke cigarettes or cigars when off-duty and in view of the passing public. They must use the Staff rest area for such purposes.

No gratuities may be accepted from parents.

Santas shall adopt an appropriate tone of voice and demeanor when addressing children. They shall not use low, slang expressions. Nor shall they, on pain of instant dismissal, abuse either verbally or physically any child or guardian.

Should an emergency occur, such as a child losing control or being sick over a Santa, then a relief will assume his duties without delay. Will you please ensure that adequate Santa relief is available at all times?

WEiRD Trees

Lights, Tinsel… ACTION

Tree Worship

How did chopping down a fir tree become a traditional way to celebrate the birth of Jesus?

Bringing greenery into the home during the shortest days of the year can be traced back to ancient Egypt, where people brought green palm fronds inside. During the pagan festival of Saturnalia, Romans decorated buildings with pine, holly, and ivy. In ancient Germany, pagan tribes in the Black Forest regarded *tannenbaum* (fir trees) as fertility symbols because their leaves thrived in the cold winter months, as if by magic.

The Church forbade the use of greenery during early Christian celebrations because of its close association with those pagan rituals. In A.D. 575, Bishop Martin of Bracae in Germany banned the use of all greenery during Christmas. In 601, Pope Gregory instructed Augustine of Canterbury to follow the custom of decking pagan temples with greenery by decorating churches in the same festive way, to commandeer pagan practices.

As early as 700, Germans placed a tree in their homes during the winter solstice. According to legend, British monk and missionary St. Boniface, determined to prove to a group of German Druids outside the town of Geismar that their sacred oak tree was not divine, chopped one down. The oak fell, crushing everything but a small fir sapling. Boniface declared the surviving fir tree a miracle worthy of the baby Jesus, starting a tradition of planting fir saplings to celebrate Christmas. (This story may very well be a literary invention meant to Christianize a pagan practice.)

By the sixteenth century, Germans were decorating fir trees for Christmas with apples, wafers, gilt, and roses cut from colored paper. In that era, Martin Luther is credited as being the first person to put candles on a tree in his home at Christmas to simulate the twinkling stars of the heavens.

The tradition of the *Christbaum* ("Christ tree") spread to other Western countries. In 1840, Prince Albert, who had German roots, married England's Queen Victoria and the couple set up a Christmas tree in Windsor Castle, popularizing the custom in the United Kingdom. Hessian mercenaries paid by the British to fight in the Revolutionary War and German settlers in Pennsylvania brought the custom to the

Treason

According to *The Guinness Book of World Records,* "The world's tallest cut Christmas tree was a 221-foot Douglas fir (Pseudotsuga menziesii) erected at Northgate Shopping Center, Seattle, Washington, in December 1950."

United States. In 1880, Woolworth's sold the first mass-produced Christmas tree ornaments.

In 1882, Edward Johnson, one of Thomas Edison's employees, lit up a Christmas tree in New York City with a string of eighty small electric light bulbs, which he went on to mass-produce around 1890. By 1900, department stores started using the new Christmas lights for their displays. Three years later, the Ever-Ready Company of New York began mass production of strings of electric lights.

In 1923, President Calvin Coolidge ceremoniously flipped the switch to illuminate the first electric lights on an outdoor Christmas tree at the White House, launching that annual tradition.

Today, Germans decorate Christmas trees with painted eggshells, and people throughout the world decorate their trees with silver tinsel (to simulate icicles), festive ornaments, candy canes, flashing lights, and an angel or a star mounted at the top to represent the star of Bethlehem.

Tinsel Time

Invented in Germany around 1610, tinsel was originally made from silver by machines that stretched the precious metal into wafer-thin strips.

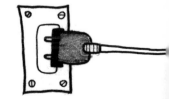

Enlightenment

The warning found on a package of 100 Super Bright Set Christmas tree lights reads: "To avoid fire and electric shock, do not install on trees having needles, leaves, or branch coverings that look like metal." So much for stringing lights on the pine tree you just spray-painted metallic silver.

Have You Seen the Light?

In 1917, a tragic fire in New York City started by Christmas tree candles inspired fifteen-year-old Albert Sadacca to make strings of safety lights for Christmas trees by adapting novelty lights sold in his family's novelty store. The first year, Albert sold one hundred strings of white lights. The second year, he used different-colored bulbs, launching a multimillion-dollar business. The NOMA Electric Company, founded by Albert Sadacca and his brothers Henri and Leon, became the largest Christmas lighting company in the world.

THE WORLD'S MOST EXPENSIVE CHRISTMAS TREE

In December 2002, a Piaget store in Tokyo, Japan, set up a twenty-foot-tall Christmas tree decorated with watches and precious stones with a total value surpassing $10.8 million, including a $1.23 million watch studded with 44.13-carat diamonds. Piaget set up the tree for a special weekend sale for invitation-only customers in the hopes of getting the tree into The Guinness Book of World Records.

RENT-A-TREE

If you want to celebrate Christmas without chopping down a tree, The Original Living Christmas Tree Company in Portland, Oregon, rents out living evergreens and then replants them after the holidays.

Company founder John Fogel and his crew dig up the living trees along with their roots, puts them in pots, and deliver them to customers in the Portland area. In 2004, Fogel rented out 419 trees, starting at $55 for a seven-foot-tall Douglas fir.

After New Year's Day, Fogel and his team return to pick up the trees, which they deliver to parks, schools, and other organizations that pay roughly $10 to have them planted on their property.

Fogel, who founded his company in 1992, only accepts orders for trees for which he has buyers willing to replant in January. As of 2005, the National Christmas Tree Association did not know of any other rent-a-Christmas-tree businesses in the United States.

Deck the Halls with Garbage?

In 1990, the 25-foot-tall Christmas tree standing on the top deck of the USNS Mercy, a hospital ship stationed in the Persian Gulf during Operation Desert Shield, was delivered from Manila on a garbage-collection barge.

Save the Trees

To prevent the annual massacre of approximately 27 million Christmas trees in the United States, and the resulting disposal problems, environmental groups urge people to buy living potted fir trees that can be replanted outside after the holiday season or donated as a tax write-off. In 2004, Americans bought 27.1 million live trees (including living potted trees) and 9 million reusable artificial trees. Live trees can be recycled and turned into mulch. Artificial trees last an average of six years.

A Tree for All Seasons

In December 2004, a church and a synagogue in Los Angeles teamed up to let Christmas trees do double duty-first for Christmas and then for the Jewish holiday of Tu B'Shevat (which Jews celebrate by planting trees). Fifty Christian and fifty Jewish families contributed $36 each to jointly purchase one tree, for a total of fifty living trees. On December 12, the living trees were delivered to the Westwood Hills Congregational Church of the United Church of Christ during a joint celebration with members of Beth Shir Shalom Temple. On January 9, the church members delivered the trees to the synagogue members, to care for the trees for three weeks until January 30, when both the Jewish and Christian families planted the trees in a public park to celebrate Tu B'Shevat.

THERE'S SOMETHING IN THE AIR

Approximately one million acres of Christmas trees are grown each year in the United States, producing enough daily oxygen for 18 million people—until they are chopped down, of course.

O Mangobaum!

In India, Christians decorate mango and banana trees.

Fruity Festivities

Instead of having Christmas trees, Italians decorate small wooden pyramids with fruit.

WHAT'S THE POINSETTIA?

In 1828, Joel Roberts Poinsett, the first ambassador to Mexico, brought a Mexican plant all yellow flowers surrounded by larger red and green leaves (Euphorbia pulcherrima) to the United States. The plant, called "flower of the blessed night" (because it resembled the Star of Bethlehem), was renamed in honor of Poinsett and quickly became a popular decoration for Christmas. If eaten, the poisonous leaves and stems of the poinsettia can cause severe abdominal cramps.

The Eternal Question:
Real Trees vs. Fake Trees

The National Christmas Tree Association argues that artificial trees rob the spirit from Christmas, are mainly manufactured in China, and cannot be recycled. Genuine trees, they insist, offer fragrance, freshness, "the look and feel of the holidays," and are a recyclable, renewable resource.

Proponents of artificial trees argue that they are lush, convenient, reusable, don't shed needles on the floor, can be purchased with lights already hung, and provide an excellent alternative to live trees that have been banned from apartment and commercial buildings due to fire-safety concerns.

As of 2005, the average price of a real tree was $42.60, compared with $68.80 for a fake one (which usually comes with a ten-year warranty).

Gas-Guzzling Christmas Trees

Strapping a Christmas tree to the top of a sport-utility vehicle creates 26 percent more aerodynamic drag, according to engineers at the University of Vermont. While the impact per vehicle is modest, the combined effect means that Americans use an additional 53,000 gallons of gas each year to lug Christmas trees home. In 2004, that added up to approximately $100,000-worth of gasoline.

GOT A TREE?

Ninety-four percent of Americans celebrate Christmas. Of those households, 88 percent put up a Christmas tree. In other words, 83 percent of all American homes have a Christmas tree.

Among Americans who put up a Christmas tree, 58 percent use an artificial tree, according to a 2004 ABC News/ *Washington Post* poll.

Affluent Americans are more apt to buy live Christmas trees. Fifty percent of Americans with household incomes over $75,000 buy live trees, while 66 percent of Americans with household incomes under $20,000 buy artificial trees.

People with post-graduate degrees are more likely to use live trees.

Sixty-eight percent use artificial trees in Southern and Midwestern states, while only 44 percent go artificial in Northeastern states, and 40 percent in Western states.

As of 2000, 32 million households put up real trees and 50.6 million households displayed an artificial one.

A 2004 consumer survey by the National Christmas Tree Association revealed that of the 36.1 million Americans who bought Christmas trees, 27.1 million bought live Christmas trees and 9 million bought artificial Christmas trees.

Rigging Up the Christmas Tree

The series of control valves at the top of an offshore oil drilling well, used to control the flow of oil, is called a "Christmas tree" because of its many branchlike fittings.

Color Coded

The traditional colors of Christmas are green and red. Green represents the belief in eternal life through Jesus. Red represents the blood shed by Jesus at his crucifixion.

THOU SHALT NOT HAVE A CHRISTMAS TREE?

In the Bible, the prophet Jeremiah states, "This is what the Lord says: 'Do not learn the way of the nations....For the customs of the peoples are worthless; they cut a tree out of the forest, and a craftsman shapes it with his chisel. They adorn it with silver and gold; they fasten it with hammer and nails so it will not totter. Like a scarecrow in a melon patch, their idols cannot speak; they must be carried because they cannot walk. Do not fear them; they can do no harm nor can they do any good.'"

Does this verse suggest that the Christmas tree custom is a form of idolatry? Or is Jeremiah simply warning the Israelites against worshipping idols carved from trees?

THE MIRACLE OF
A CHRISTMAS CALAMITY

Christopher Radko, the acclaimed designer of keepsake mouth-blown, hand-painted, glass Christmas ornaments, got into business completely by accident. In 1984, Radko replaced his family's rusty Christmas tree stand with a brand-new aluminum stand, set up a 14-foot tree, and decorated it with his family's collection of more than 2,000 mouth-blown, European glass ornaments. A week before Christmas, the new stand collapsed and the tree fell to the floor, shattering nearly every ornament.

Determined to replace the ornaments so precious to his family, Radko visited cousins in Poland and began searching for classic glass ornaments. He failed to find superior-quality ones, but he did find a man eager to revive the glass-blowing art of his great-grandfather. With Radko's encouragement, the man recovered antique ornament molds and created ornaments from Radko's sketches of his childhood favorites and new designs from his own imagination. The man produced several dozen ornaments, but before Radko ever got to hang them on his family's tree, his friends in New York insisted on buying them.

Radko made another trip to Poland and brought back more ornaments for his family and friends, who encouraged him to get them distributed in stores. While working in the mailroom of a New York City talent agency, Radko spent his lunch hours going door-to-door to stores in Manhattan, showing his ornaments and designs. Before long, Radko's company grew from a lone glass-blower to more than 3,000 people commissioned in cottage workshops in Poland, Germany, Italy, and the Czech Republic.

The Christmas Spider

Ukrainians decorate Christmas trees with an artificial spider and web. Ukrainian legend holds that tinsel originated when a spider wove cobwebs all over a Christmas tree at night and the rising sun turned it to silver. Finding a real spider web on Christmas morning is considered good luck.

THE CHRISTMAS TREE THAT ATE PITTSBURGH

On February 18, 2000, Warren Wynne of Pittsburgh, Pennsylvania, finally got around to taking down his Christmas tree. Too lazy to carry the tree downstairs to the curb for pickup, thirty-one-year-old Wynne hurled the tree out the window of his sixth-floor apartment, hitting a power line and knocking out electricity for about four hundred customers.

The Largest Live Christmas Tree in the World

The Christmas tree at New York City's Rockefeller Center is the biggest, brightest, and most famous Christmas tree on earth.

The tradition of the Rockefeller Center Christmas tree began in 1931, during the construction of the complex. Two years later, a Christmas tree strung with 700 lights was formally placed in front of the RCA Building at 30 Rockefeller Plaza. In 1936, an outdoor ice skating rink was constructed in front of the RCA Building. NBC-TV first televised the Rockefeller Center Christmas tree lighting in 1951 on *The Kate Smith Show*. From 1953 to 1955, the network broadcast the annual tree lighting as part of *The Howdy Doody Show*.

The Rockefeller Center Christmas tree is nearly always a Norway spruce, usually over fifty years old and at least 65 feet tall and 35 feet wide, although the trees usually stand from 75 to 90 feet tall. Every year just after the Thanksgiving holiday weekend, the tree travels along a carefully planned route with a police escort in the middle of the night, to disrupt as little traffic as possible. The farthest distance a tree has ever traveled was some 518 miles—from Ottawa, Canada. Rockefeller Plaza employees decorate the tree with 30,000 lights attached to five miles of wire.

Oriental Ornaments

The Chinese decorate Christmas trees with paper lanterns.

MAY YOUR DAYS BE MERRY...
AND VERY, VERY BRIGHT

Where can you see the most outrageous Christmas light displays in the United States?

- **Al Copeland Residence:** Every year since 1974, Al Copeland, the founder of Popeyes Chicken, has decorated his home in Metairie, Louisiana, with thousands of lights for the holiday season. Airline pilots passing overhead often point it out to passengers.

- **Austin's 37th Street:** Ever since the 1980s, the residents of West 37th Street near Guadalupe Street in Austin, Texas, have decorated their homes with a profusion of lights, creating one of the most zany and concentrated arrays of residential Christmas decorations in the United States. Imagine an enormous Texas flag of lights, a flickering bicycle and mannequin hanging from a tree, Barney the dinosaur tied to railroad tracks, and a Volkswagen illuminated with lights inside and out.

- **Bill Clot Residence:** In 2002, NBC's *Today* show declared the home of aircraft parts distributor Bill Clot the most spectacular outdoor Christmas display in the nation. The Clot house in Pinecrest, Florida, features 600,000 lights, live Christmas trees, and 110 animated figures, including a Nativity scene with a waving baby Jesus and nodding camels, ice-skating penguins, an animal rock band, figurines from the Nutcracker Suite, singing carolers, busy elves, wide-eyed children, a carousel, grazing reindeer, and multiple Santas.

- **Domino's Farms:** Drive your car through Domino's Farms in Ann Arbor Michigan, sponsored by Domino's Pizza founder Tom Monaghan, to see more than a million lights. Then come inside to have your photograph taken with Santa Claus and see an around-the-world Nativity exhibit, decorated trees, and a gingerbread village. You can top it all off by taking a miniature train ride.

- **Dyker Heights:** Between 10th and 12th Avenues on 84th Street in Dyker Heights, Brooklyn, three families decorate their homes to excess, including 29-foot-tall toy soldiers, animatronic galloping horses, dancers pirouetting to the Nutcracker Suite, life-size characters from the 1970 movie *Scrooge*, motorized dolls, miniature villages, fabled creatures, and illuminated soldiers. The display attracts 150,000 visitors a year.

- **Leavenworth Village Lighting Festival:** Every year since 1969, the Bavarian-themed village of Leavenworth, Washington, transforms itself into a Village of Lights, festooned with thousands of twinkling lights throughout the holidays. Up to 40,000 visitors attend the Christmas Lighting Festival, which features music, dancing, German foods, and a lantern parade.

- **Martin and Andrew Lindsay Residence:** In 2000, mechanical engineer Martin Lindsay and his brother, electrical engineer Andrew Lindsay, designed and installed a computerized lightshow synchronized to music at their parent's house in Thornhill, Ontario. Every year since then, the display has grown increasingly elaborate. The repeating five-minute light show features more than 15,000 hand-strung colored lights, and the music is broadcast over FM radio.

- **Mission Inn:** More than 2 million lights adorn this historic landmark hotel in downtown Riverside, California. The annual event known as the Festival of Lights begins the day after Thanksgiving at a switch-on ceremony that attracts an estimated 20,000 people.

- **Motor Speedway Christmas:** Each year during the holiday season the city of Bristol, Tennessee, holds its Christmas light display at the Bristol Motor Speedway, where visitors drive a lap around the official NASCAR track to view "Speedway in Lights" with more than 1.5 million lights. The 200-plus displays include a Dinosaur Village with an erupting volcano and six dinosaurs.

- **Newport Beach Boat Parade:** Hailed as "one of the top ten holiday happenings in the nation" by the *New York Times*, the Annual Newport Harbor Christmas Boat Parade in California sets the harbor ablaze for five consecutive nights as the owners of yachts, boats, kayaks, and canoes try to outdo one another with unique lighting displays accompanied by music and costumed carolers.
- **Rich Faucher Residence:** In 1980, Boeing helicopter factory worker Rich Faucher began decorating his home in New Castle, Delaware, with a massive array of lights for Christmas. Today, the Faucher home boasts one of the largest private Christmas light displays in the country, featuring 602,000 colored lights, an 8-foot-tall motor-operated Christmas carousel, a snow bunny teeter-totter, a motorized train, a thirty-piece choir, six 12-foot-tall Christmas stockings, 114 blow-molds, 126 strobe lights, eight inflatable figures, an animated Santa with elves in his workshop, a life-size Nativity scene, and lighted arches-most of which are handmade.

   Visitors to the Faucher home can shakes hands with live characters, including Frosty the Snowman, Rudolph the Red-Nosed Reindeer, Dancing Ca ndy Canes, and Santa's Elves. Every child gets to sit on Santa's lap and

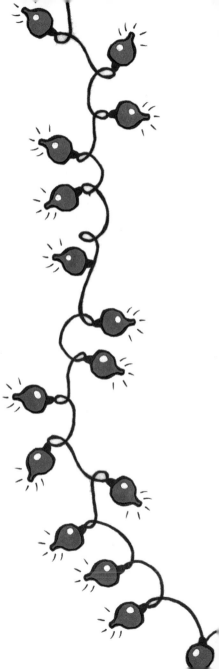

receives a candy cane and a small gift—all free of charge.

- **Ron Lister Residence:** In 1989, Ron Lister built a computerized light display at his house in Kissimmee, Florida, that has grown to feature 40,000 lights synchronized to music that is transmitted by radio (so guests can listen to the music from the comfort of their cars). The entire lighting display, choreographed to four songs, runs seventeen minutes. Ron handmade all the large elements in his display, including a blinking star of Bethlehem, large flickering snowflakes, a glittering "Season's Greetings" sign, illuminated large gift-wrapped Christmas packages, a glittering star field behind a Nativity Scene, deer drinking from a pond, and several large palm trees.
- **Silver Dollar City:** During the holiday season, the Silver Dollar City theme park in Branson, Missouri, ignites 4 million lights and one thousand decorated Christmas trees, including a dramatic five-story Special Effects Tree, that glows with more than 250,000 lights synchronized to Christmas songs. Silver Dollar City also features a Holiday Light Parade, an elaborate stage production of Charles Dickens's *A Christmas Carol*, a re-creation of the ancient town of Bethlehem, and a Living Nativity staged in a two-story theater-in-the-round.
- **Trinity Broadcasting Network:** Every year the Trinity Broadcasting Network decorates its Trinity Christian City International headquarters in Costa Mesa, California, with 1 million bright lights, prompting protests from neighboring residents.
- **Winterfest in the Smokies:** Every year since 1974, the Tennessee cities of Gatlinburg, Pigeon Forge, and Sevierville team up to create an outrageous Christmas light display featuring millions of lights arranged in festive themes, and kicked off with a Fantasy of Lights Christmas Parade, which, in 2002, featured nearly 1,000 cheerleaders.
- **Wonderland of Lights:** Since 1987, the town of Marshall, Texas, transforms into a Wonderland of Lights for six weeks every holiday season. More than 7 million tiny white lights decorate the historic courthouse, the entire business district, and area neighborhoods, attracting more than 200,000 visitors.
- **World's Largest Salvation Army Kettle:** Every holiday season, the world's largest Salvation Army kettle, illuminated with more than 20,000 lights, stands in Ecolab Plaza in downtown St. Paul, Minnesota.

Singing Christmas Tree

Every year at St. Francis de Sales church in Muskegon, Michigan, three hundred singers from the Mona Shores High School Choir stand on tiers on a 53-foot-tall steel structure shaped like a Christmas tree and decorated with greenery, bows, garlands, and thousands of lights to perform a two-hour seasonal serenade. A smaller version of the Mona Shores Singing Christmas Tree once traveled to Washington D.C., where twenty-five members of the choir sang at the White House.

Deck the Garbage

Every October, workers at the Rumpke Landfill outside Cincinnati, Ohio, string 30,000 Christmas lights on top of the mound of garbage that covers 234 acres of land and rises 279 feet above street level. The display includes 25-foot-tall candy canes.

ALUMINUM TREE MUSEUM

The Aluminum Tree and Aesthetically Challenged Seasonal Ornament Museum and Research Center in Brevard, North Carolina, displays more than thirty Christmas trees made from aluminum and decorated in various themes, including the "Elvis Tree" with photos of the King, the "Toilet Tree" (adorned with pink, yellow and blue shower curtain connectors), and the "Bing Crosby Tree'" (covered with silver bells). Visitors can also purchase aluminum tree seeds and seedlings.

Yule
Days

The ancient Scandinavians kindled huge bonfires in honor of the winter solstice. They believed that the Yule log, a tree trunk large enough to burn throughout the longest winter night, helped usher in the return of the sun. The ancients also believed that the ashes from the Yule log had magical powers to cure maladies, fertilize fields, and protect a house against lightning. Families often carved an oak Yule log into a decorative block which they placed on the floor of their hearth. Today, many people keep an unburned piece of the log to light the next years' log. The word Yule is believed to stem from the from the Middle English word Yollen, meaning "to cry aloud," because when early Anglo-Saxons discovered that nights were becoming shorter again, they yelled with glee.

Will the Real "Christmas Tree Capital of the World" Please Stand Up?

Clackamas County, Oregon, calls itself "The Christmas Tree Capital of the World." So does Avery County, North Carolina; Missaukee County, Michigan; and Indiana County, Pennsylvania (the birthplace of Jimmy Stewart, star of the classic Christmas movie, *It's a Wonderful Life*).

Not even the National Christmas Tree Association, a St. Louis-based professional trade group that annually selects the official White House Christmas tree, has declared which county leads the national Christmas tree harvest. So which is it?

According to the 2002 USDA National Agricultural Statistics Service report, the top twenty producers of Christmas trees in the United States are:

1. Clackamas County, Oregon: 2.59 million
2. Benton County, Oregon: 1.4 million
3. Marion County, Oregon: 1.03 million
4. Ashe County, North Carolina: 876,194
5. Avery County, North Carolina: 848,113
6. Missaukee County, Michigan: 654,011
7. Waushara County, Wisconsin: 641,921
8. Alleghany County, North Carolina: 427,954
9. Lewis County, Washington: 412,225
10. Wexford County, Michigan: 365,184
11. Jackson County, Wisconsin: 255,898
12. Washington County, Oregon: 253,695
13. Oceana County, Michigan: 220,566
14. Montcalm County, Michigan: 213,350
15. Jackson County, North Carolina: 202,752
16. Grayson County, Virginia: 190,895
17. Pine County, Minnesota: 171,617
18. Watauga County, North Carolina: 166,846
19. Lane County, Oregon: 151,897
20. Indiana County, Pennsylvania: 149,896

Mistletoe Weirdness

In the second century B.C., the highest-ranking Druid priest in England used a gold knife to cut mistletoe, an evergreen plant that grows as a parasite on the trunks and branches of various trees, from sacred oak trees. People burned the mistletoe as a sacrifice to their gods, wore sprigs of it as charms, hung it in their homes to ensure good fortune and family harmony, and embraced under a sprig of the yellow-green plant with white berries. The Druids also hung mistletoe outside their homes as a sign of peace and welcome to strangers.

Like the Druids, Norse Vikings hung mistletoe outside their homes to welcome strangers. In Norse mythology, the giant Loki threw an arrow made of mistletoe at the beloved god Balder, son of the chief god Odin and the goddess Frigga, piercing his heart and killing him. Frigga had made all animals, plants, and stones swear an oath not to harm Balder, but she overlooked one plant—the mistletoe. Hel, the goddess of the dead, insisted that Balder could be resurrected if all things wept for him. Everything wept for Balder—except the giant Loki. Consequently, Balder must remain dead until Ragnarok, a great battle in which the world will be destroyed by fire. Norse legend holds that a better world will rise from the ashes and Balder will return from the dead to rule over it—a surprising parallel to the Christian concept of the Second Coming.

The custom of kissing under the mistletoe has been traced back to the Roman Saturnalia and certain primitive marriage rites, but the

practice seems to have survived only in English-speaking countries. In England, the Christmas mistletoe is superstitiously burned on Twelfth Night out of fear that boys and girls who have kissed under it might otherwise never marry.

Since mistletoe had been associated with pagan rituals, throughout the Middle Ages the church prohibited Christians from using the plant in any way. Instead, the church advocated making wreaths from holly, whose sharp, pointed leaves resemble the crown of thorns worn by Jesus at his crucifixion and whose red berries signify drops of his blood. Not exactly the merriest symbol to tack to your front door to celebrate the festive season.

WEIRD
Traditions
Flaming Pants, Elephant Consommé, and Christmas Pickles

Bad Hair Day

In Sweden, the Christmas season begins on St. Lucia's Day, celebrated on December 13. In the morning, the oldest daughter in the home dresses in white, wears a wreath with seven lit candles on her head, and serves her family coffee and buns in bed—ideally without setting her head on fire.

How do you say "merry christmas?"

Afghan
Christmas-e-Shoma Mobarak

Akan
Afishara

Afrikaans
Geseënde Kersfees

Albanian
Gezur Krislinjden

No Vacancy

On December 16, Mexicans begin nine days of candlelight parades to reenact Mary and Joseph's search for a room, followed every night by parties and the breaking of piñatas.

Invasion of the Party Crashers

In Ireland, two weeks before Christmas, men and pipers go from house to house, dancing and serenading the occupants.

Sun Worship

In Australia and New Zealand, many people celebrate Christmas by going to the beach.

Amharic
Enkwan laberhana
ledat abaqqawot

Arabic
Mboni Chrismen

Armenian
Shenoraavor Nor
Dari yev Pari
gagland

Azeri
Tezze Illinez Yahsi
Olsum

Bangla
Shuvo Baro Din

Bantu
Na Bino Banso
Bonane

Belarusian
Winshuyu sa
Svytakami

Bengal
Shuvo Naba Barsha

Brahui
Arkas caik xuda are

Bulgarian
Tchestito Rojestvo
Hristovo

Catalan
Bon Nadal

The Greatest Nativity Show on Earth

The Marian Library, at the University of Dayton in Ohio, houses the largest collection of Nativity sets in the United States, consisting of nearly 1,000 creative, diverse, and nontraditional crèches, representing cultures from fifty-one countries on six continents.

All of the Nativity sets include figures of Joseph, Mary, and the baby Jesus, but some in the vast collection also feature polar bears, armadillos, flying camels, mariachi musicians, cooks, and toy makers. The sets—varying in size, color scheme, and complexity—range from traditional to imaginative, from solemn to comical. Some are made with gravel, foliage, cork, bamboo, and moss. Others incorporate bread, wax, and clothespins. The manger scenes are set in a forest, desert, mountaintop, cave, a Swiss chalet, and the center of a Mexican village.

The library began amassing its vast collection of varied cultural interpretations of the Nativity in 1994. Every year during the holiday season it displays a large array of Nativity sets at several venues in Dayton, Ohio, and on the Internet at www.udnativity.org. Many of the Nativities can be seen year round on permanent display in the library.

HOLIDAY SWEEPSTAKES

On Christmas Eve, Norwegians hide all the brooms in the house to prevent witches and mischievous spirits from stealing them and going for a ride.

Unruly Ruler

In the British armed forces, officers serve Christmas dinner to the lower ranks. The tradition originated during Saturnalia in Rome, where slaves became equals with their masters. When the Normans invaded England in 1066, they introduced into the Christmas festivities a red-robed mock king called the Lord of Misrule, whose job was to ensure that the celebrations were conducted in the ribald pagan style. In the Middle Ages, an English master would allow his servants to elect their own ruler of the holiday. This Lord of Misrule would preside over a great banquet at which the master would wait on all the servants, resulting in festive revelry. The English traditions of wearing paper hats and setting off firecrackers are also reminiscent of the wilder excesses of ancient Rome.

Creole
Bonn e Erez Ane

Croatian
Sretan Bozic

Czech
Prejeme Vam Vesele Vanoce

Danish
Glaedelig Jul

Dutch
Froleijk Kerstfeest

English
Merry Christmas

DING-A-LINGS

In Switzerland, the Christmas season commences with a whip-cracking contest, followed on December 4 by a parade of two hundred men and women dressed in white robes, some wearing big bells around their necks.

Viva los Nacimientos

Toward the holiday season, the local market in Tonala, Mexico, features dozens of stalls that sell nothing but supplies and accessories for Nativity scenes, called *nacimientos* in Spanish. Traditionally, the elaborate nacimientos, which the people constantly improve by adding more characters and scenes each year, serve as the primary decorations in local homes, businesses, and churches in Tonala.

Mexicans use moss, sawdust, sand, and painted paper to create hills, deserts, rivers, and lakes. They build entire villages on tabletops, with wells, vendors with carts of fruits and vegetables, playing children, musicians, dancers, mutton and pork roasting on spits, and women making tortillas. Uniquely Mexican touches include the rooster who crowed to announce the birth of the baby Jesus, fish in the river (from the Mexican Christmas carol of the same name—"Los Peces en el Rio"), Lucifer lurking in his cave to tempt the shepherds from their journey, and Egyptians camping with their tents and pyramids.

Estonian
Ruumsaid Juulupjji

Ewe
Blunya na wo

Filipino
Maligayang Pasko

Finn
Hauskaa Joulua

Fisian
Noflike Krystdagen

Flemish
Zalig Kerstfeest

French
Joyeux Noel

Ga
Afi o! Afi!

Gaelic
Nollaig Shona Dhuit

Georgian
Gilotsavt Kristes

A Picture-Perfect Christmas

Every Christmas season, American parents spend between $9 and $30 for a photograph of their child sitting on Santa's lap, earning millions for the companies that stage the Santa photo shoots.

The Santa Claus at each one of the nation's 1,800 malls attracts an average of 7,720 children each year, according to figures from the International Council of Shopping Centers.

The three leading Santa photo companies in the United States are Cherry Hill Photo Enterprises of Cherry Hill, New Jersey, SantaPlus of St. Peters, Missouri, and Noerr Programs Corporation of Golden, Colorado. The companies typically rent a prominent space in the mall and provide the Santa, sets, cameras, and photographers.

Cherry Hill Photo Enterprises, founded in 1961, places roughly 1,000 Santas in 400 malls. SantaPlus, founded in 1984, places Santas in more than 300 malls across the United States. Noerr Programs Corporation, founded in 1989, places some 200 Santas in 150 locations. All three companies require their Santas to go through a criminal background check and a drug test.

The companies estimate that 40 to 85 percent of adults who bring children to see Santa buy at least one photo, spending an average of $17. That adds up to an estimated $35 million worth of photos every year.

German
Frohliche
Weihnachten

Greek
Kala Christougenna

Greenlandic
Juullimi pilluaritsi

Hawaiian
Mele Kalikimaka

Hebrew
Mo'adim Lesimkha

Hindi
Sub Naya Baras

Hungarian
Kellemes Karacsonyi
Unnnepeket

Icelandic
Gledileg Joi

Indonesian
Selamat Hari Natal

Italian
Buon Natale

Japanese
Meri Kurisumasu

FLOOR IT

In Bulgaria, people traditionally place straw on the floor of their homes to re-create the feeling of the manger.

Baby Talk

Italians decorate their homes with a *presepio*, an artistically decorated crib for baby Jesus

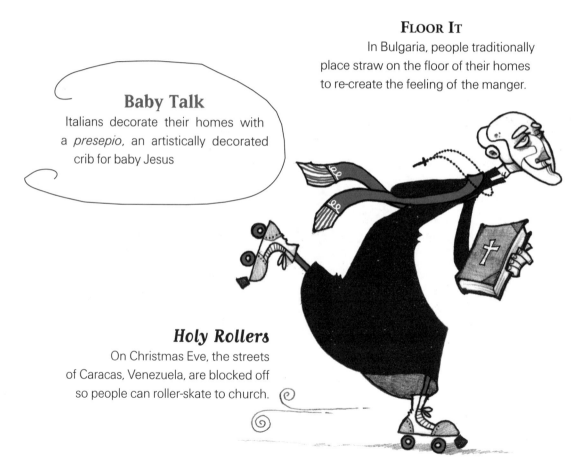

Holy Rollers

On Christmas Eve, the streets of Caracas, Venezuela, are blocked off so people can roller-skate to church.

Kazakh
Hristos Razdajetsja

Kinyarwanda
Umunsi Mwiza

Kiswahili
Krismas Njema

Korean
Sung Tan Chuk Ha

Kurdish
Seva piroz sahibe u
sersala te piroz be

Making a List

In Spain, after midnight Mass (called Mass of the Rooster), people dance and sing in the streets. On December 28, Spaniards commemorate the day of Holy Innocents (when King Herod ordered the killing of the baby Jesus) by holding a Fool's Festival and electing a mayor from among the young boys to publicly read a list of complaints about people in the town.

The Birth of Nativity Scenes

Historians credit St. Francis of Assisi with creating the first Nativity scene in a real stable in 1223. St. Francis used local Italian people and barnyard animals to restage the birth of Jesus. In the seventeenth and eighteenth centuries, Capuchin, Jesuit, and Franciscan orders in Italy, France, southern Germany, and Austria promoted and popularized handcrafted replicas of the Nativity scene.

GOING DUTCH

The Pennsylvania Dutch (descendants of German settlers in the United States) set up a hand-carved Nativity scene of baby Jesus in the manger, called a *Putz*.

In Yiddish, the word *putz* is slang for "penis".

Christmas in Cuba

In December 1997, Cuban dictator Fidel Castro allowed Cubans to celebrate Christmas, giving them the day off for the first time in twenty-eight years, to demonstrate his goodwill before Pope John Paul II's five-day visit to the island nation scheduled for the following January.

After Cuba's 1959 communist revolution, the Castro regime nationalized the church's properties, closed its schools, and tortured and jailed members of the clergy. Three years later, the government adopted atheism as official doctrine and branded anyone associated with Christianity a counterrevolutionary.

In 1969, Castro banned public recognition of Christmas and required all citizens to work on Christmas Day, supposedly to increase sugar production. He never lifted the ban. Christmas celebrations went underground. The Cuban government legalized religious worship in 1991, but few Cubans, fearful of government recrimination, practiced their religion publicly.

The pope met with Castro during his 1998 visit, and Castro attended the pope's Mass held in Havana's Revolution Square.

Today, the average Cuban celebrates Christmas modestly by decorating a small tree and enjoying a meal of roast pork and beer. Cubans tend to celebrate more boisterously on New Year's, the anniversary of the day in 1959 when Fidel Castro's rebels marched into Havana. The Castro regime must approve any public Christmas displays, and consequently, very little Christmas cheer is permitted outside the church. A huge Christmas tree does grace the lobby of most tourist hotels, and a lighted Christmas tree topped with a gold star stands inside the 300-year-old Iglesia Santo Cristo del Buen Viaje, a church near Havana harbor, but decorated trees are rarely seen in other public places around the city. There aren't any Christmas parades in Cuba. the signs on department store walls wish *"Feliz Ano"* (Happy New Year) rather than *"Feliz Navidad"* (Merry Christmas), and stores and hotels do not pipe in Christmas carols and songs.

Latin
Natale hilare

Latvian
Prieci'gus
Ziemsve'tkus

Lithuanian
Linksmu Kaledu

Sounds Greek to Me
During the twelve days of Christmas, Greeks burn herbs in the fireplace to prevent mischievous goblins, called *kallikantzeri*, from dropping down the chimney to extinguish the fire or sour the milk. Hanging a basil-wrapped cross over a bowl of water is also supposed to help ward off the *kallikantzeri*, as will leaving chunks of meat outside the door as a bribe.

What Is Boxing Day?
In the United Kingdom, Australia, New Zealand, and parts of Canada, the day after Christmas is a national holiday called Boxing Day, which has nothing to do with the sport of boxing (or punch of any kind). On Boxing Day, people give monetary gifts in small boxes to tradespeople, servants, and minor public officials—a custom which may have begun in ancient Rome. Originally, apprentices collected contributions from customers in an earthenware Christmas box. Once filled, the box was broken and the contents were shared—which, if done improperly, could cause an outburst of spontaneous amateur boxing.

Luganda
Amazalibwa
Agesanyu

Macedonian
Streken Bozhik

Madagasy
Arahaba Tratry ny Krismasy

Malay
Selamat Hri Krimas

The Christmas Pickle

An urban legend insists that the custom of hiding a Christmas pickle ornament deep in the branches of the family Christmas tree on Christmas Eve is an old German tradition. Supposedly, the first person to find the pickle ornament on Christmas morning receives an extra gift or good luck for the entire coming year. While several American companies sell pickle-shaped glass ornaments, no such tradition exists in Germany. The story seems to have been contrived by someone determined to sell glass pickle ornaments.

Nepali
Krist Yesu Ko
Shuva Janma Utsav
Ko Upalaxhma
Hardik Shuva

Mandarin
Sheng Dan Kuai Le

Moldavan
Craciun Fericit si

Navajo
Merry Keshmish

Maori
Meri Kirihimete

When to Invest in Hallmark

Today, Americans exchange approximately 2 billion Christmas cards, making Christmas the number one holiday for selling greeting cards—guaranteeing crowded Hallmark stores and long lines at the post office.

LUCKY NUMBER

The average American sends thirty-eight Christmas cards every year.

Cupid Beats Santa

The first commercially produced Valentine's Day cards were printed in 1803, forty years before the first commercially produced Christmas cards.

The Night of the Radish

Every December 23, the Mexican town of Oaxaca celebrates "The Night of the Radish" to commemorate the day when Spanish colonialists brought the red-hot vegetable to Mexico in the eighteenth century. Since that time, Mexican farmers have bred radishes into misshapen vegetables the size of potatoes, inspiring Mexican artists to carve the oversized radishes into intricate figures for Nativity scenes. Every year, a prize is awarded for the best-sculpted radish, and "The Night of the Radish" culminates with fireworks.

Norwegian
God Jul

Papua
Bikpela Hamamas
Blong Dispela
Krismas

Pashtu
Christmas Aao
Ne-way Kaal Mo
Mobarak Sha

Polish
Wesolych Swiat

Portuguese
Boas Festas

Punjabi
Hacahi Ke Eide

QUAYLE FOR CHRISTMAS

In 1991, Vice President Dan Quayle and his wife sent out hundreds of Christmas cards containing a misspelled word: "May our nation continue to be the beakon of hope to the world."

TEPID GREETINGS

In 1931, Hugh Troy, described as "America's leading practical joker," sent out Christmas cards with a faint design of meandering swirls, printed with nothing but a border and the ambiguous message, "Soak this card in tepid water five minutes." Many of his friends, unable to get a design or message to appear, figured they had used the wrong temperature water. Others saw images appear where nothing was meant to appear.

Romanian
Craciun Fericit

Russian
Rozhdestrom
Kristovym

Quechua
Sumaj kausay
kachun Navidad
ch'sisipi

Samoan
La Mannia Le
Kilsimasi

And the Winner Is...

According to *The Guinness Book of Records*, "The greatest number of personal Christmas cards sent by an individual is believed to be 62,824, by Werner Erhard of San Francisco, California, in December 1975." Erhard, a man who had defrauded several companies and abandoned his wife and children, founded est (Erhard Seminar Training), hosting controversial weekend retreats where paying adherents were denied food and bathrooms until they achieved self-reliance.

Scottish
Nollaig Chridheil
Huibh

Season's Greetings

In 1843, London artist John Calcott Horsley designed the first commercially printed Christmas card. The card featured an illustration of a large family enjoying a festive Christmas party and was inscribed with the words, "A Merry Christmas and a Happy New Year to You." Sir Henry Cole, the wealthy businessman who had commissioned Horsley, printed more than a thousand cards at a cost of one shilling each (the equivalent of a day's wages for the average worker). Only twelve of the original hand-colored cards exist today. The card outraged members of the British Temperance Movement, who sternly criticized Horsley for depicting children drinking wine. By 1862, the advent of cheap color lithography made printing Christmas cards affordable, giving rise to an annual ritual in England and Germany.

SAVING FACE
Never send red Christmas cards to anyone in Japan. Red is the color reserved for funeral notices.

In the United States, Richard Pease printed the first commercial Christmas card sometime between 1850 and 1852 to advertise Pease's Great Variety Store in Albany, New York. The card pictured Santa Claus and a black slave setting the Christmas dinner table. In 1875, Boston lithographer Louis Prang, a German native, became the "father of the American Christmas card" when he began printing expensive cards depicting various floral arrangements. Americans, however, preferred to send penny Christmas postcards imported from Germany and Prang went out of business in 1890. During World War I, Americans turned away from anything German, and the American greeting card industry was born.

Serbian
Hristos se rodi

Siswati
Heri ya Krismasi

Slovak
Vesele Vianoce

Slovenian
Vesele Bozhichne Praznike

Christmas

Christmas is the season of unprotected sex, according to a 1999 study conducted by researchers at the London School of Hygiene and Tropical Medicine and published in the *Journal of the Royal Society of Medicine*.

By analyzing statistics for births, abortions, incidence of STDs, and condom sales from 1990 to 1996, the researchers discovered that the birth rate peaks nine months after Christmas, especially among unmarried women. They also found that the number of abortions in the United Kingdom is highest every year between January and March, the number of

Somali
Ciid Wanaagsan
Iyo Sanad Cusub Oo
Fiican

Sotho
Matswalo a Morena
a Mabotse

Spanish
Feliz Navidad

Surinam
Zalig Kerfeest

Sinhala
Subha Nath Thalak
Vewa

Sudan
Wilujeng Natal

Excess

people being tested for sexually transmitted diseases peaks in the first three months of each new year, and condom sales reach their greatest pinnacle just before Christmas.

These findings clearly indicate an increase in unprotected sex during the holiday season, and the researcher advocated seasonal sexual health campaigns to reverse the trend.

People might be less careful during the holidays because they are often on vacation and frequently intoxicated, and fail to use condoms or other methods of birth control.

Pop Goes the Manger

In 2004, Madame Tussaud's Wax Museum in London set up a Nativity scene with President George W. Bush, British prime minister Tony Blair, and Britain's Duke of Edinburgh as the Wise Men; movie star Samuel Jackson, British actor Hugh Grant, and Irish comedian Graham Norton as the shepherds; British soccer star David Beckham as Joseph; and his wife, singer Posh Spice, as Mary.

Swazi
Sinifisela Khisimusi
Lomuhle

Swedish
God Jul

Tamil
Nathar Puthu
Varuda Valthukkal

Thai
Sawadee Pee Mai

Tigrinya
Poket Kristmet

Tongan
Kilisimasi Fiepia

Turkish
Mutlu Noeller

Urdu
Shadae Christmas

Ukrainian
Hrystos Razhdayetsa

Vietnamese
Chuc Mung Giang
Sinh

The Gift That Keeps on Giving

For twenty-five years, Larry Kunkel of Bensenville, Illinois, and his brother-in-law Roy Collette exchanged the same pair of pants as a Christmas present—and they made the gift more difficult to open each year.

It all started in 1964, when Larry's mother gave him a pair of moleskin pants. The trousers froze stiff in cold weather, so the next Christmas Larry wrapped them up nicely and gave them to his brother-in-law. Roy didn't want the pants either, so the following Christmas, he wrapped them up and gave them back to Larry, starting an annual tradition.

One year, Roy twisted the pants tightly and stuffed them into a 3-foot-long, 1-inch diameter pipe. From then on, the gift-wrapping escalated out of control, in the hope of ending the practical joke. Over the years, the pants were:

- Compressed into a 7-inch-square bale and wrapped with wire.
- Sealed inside a 2-foot-square crate filled with stones, nailed shut, and banded with steel.
- Encased inside an insulated window that came with a twenty-year guarantee.
- Stuffed into a 5-inch coffee can, which was then soldered shut and put in a 5-gallon container filled with concrete and reinforcing rods.
- Welded inside a 600-pound safe decorated with red and green stripes.
- Locked in the glove compartment of a green 1974 Gremlin automobile, which was then crushed into a three-foot cube.

In 1989, Roy decided to encase the pants in 10,000 pounds of jagged glass. As molten glass was being poured over the insulated container that held the pants, a large chunk fractured, accidentally cremating the pants. Roy placed the ashes inside a brass urn and gave it to Larry with the epitaph: "Sorry, Old Man. Here lies the Pants."

Zulu
Sinifisela Ukhisimusi
Omuhle

Welch
Nadolig Llawen

Yiddish
Gute Vaynakhtn

FENG SHUI CHRISTMAS TIPS

Feng Shui experts claim that their tips can help you transform your home into a magical place to celebrate Christmas.

Feng Shui consultant Sarah Shurety, author of *Feng Shui for Your Home* and *Quick Feng Shui Cures*, urges decorating with plenty of greenery to offset the stress produced by the abundance of "red fire" energy created by Christmas lights.

Shurety says angels and cherubs are lucky symbols that fill the room with good will and peace. When it comes to decorating the tree, gold and silver tinsel can strengthen your intuition and represent ostentation, money, and fame. Red decorations, such as ornaments and ribbons, represent deep and passionate love, warding off evil forces. Blue decorations represent spiritualism, thoughtfulness, and consideration, and have a calming effect. Feng Shui frowns upon using white decorations, such as aerosol snow for your windows, because white is the color of mourning.

Feng Shui expert Robyn Bentley, author of *Creating a Haven: Simple Steps for a Healthy and Nurturing Home*, claims that wallets, purses, and wristwatches are unlucky items to give as Christmas gifts.

Watches suggest a limited life span, and giving empty wallets or purses portends bad luck. To turn the bad luck of an empty wallet or purse into good luck, simply place a small amount of money inside.

Handkerchiefs have negative Feng Shui because they suggest that the recipient will be doing a lot of crying in the future or wiping away perspiration from frustration.

Candy makes a gift filled with positive Feng Shui and represents your sincere wishes for the recipient to have a sweet life.

Bentley strongly warns against recycling a gift you have received by giving it to another person. Doing so creates bad Feng Shui because "re-gifting" symbolizes that you are giving away your friendship with the person who gave the gift to you.

The World's Largest Christmas Store

The world's largest year-round Christmas store sits on 45 acres in Frankenmuth, Michigan. Bronner's CHRISTmas Wonderland is large enough to hold 5.5 football fields inside, and the remaining 27 acres are beautifully landscaped with more than 2,400 individual flowering and ornamental plants. Outside the store stand three giant Santas towering 17 feet tall, a giant snowman rising 15 feet high, and a life-size Nativity scene featuring twenty-four figures. Every evening, approximately 100,000 lights illuminate Bronner's half-mile-long Christmas Lane. Bronner's electrical bill averages $900 per day. In 1985, AAA of Michigan listed Bronner's CHRISTmas Wonderland among the top ten man-made attractions in the state.

It all began by accident. In 1951, Wallace Bronner, a window display designer for a hardware store in Bay City, Michigan, met several merchants from a nearby town who were seeking Christmas decorations for their city lampposts. Wally designed and produced Christmas panels for the town, launching a career by providing Christmas decorations to communities, shopping centers, and stores.

In 1954, Wally and his wife, Irene, opened a store in Frankenmuth, Michigan, on property owned by his maternal ancestors. Wally's father, a skilled stonemason, did much of the construction work himself.

The store featured decorations for cities and shopping centers, plus gifts and trims for the home in religious, traditional, and Toyland themes. The business quickly snowballed. Wally and Irene bought the nearby Frankenmuth Bank Building in 1966 and converted it into a second store called the Tannenbaum Shop. Five years later, the Bronners purchased a nearby grocery store and turned it into a third store called Bronner's Bavarian Corner. Business continued to boom, so in 1977, the Bronners consolidated the three stores into one location on a 45-acre tract of land on the south side of Frankenmuth. The city christened the new street address 25 Christmas Lane.

In 1991, the Bronners nearly doubled the size of the store. The following year, with permission from the government of Austria, the Bronners built a replica of the

Oberndorf Silent Night Memorial Chapel (where the Christmas carol "Silent Night" was played for the first time on Christmas Eve in 1818) as a tribute to the hymn, and displayed a verse of the song in over three hundred languages on the chapel grounds. In 2001, the Bronners expanded the building yet again.

Today, the store offers more than 50,000 different items, including five hundred different types of Nativity scenes (including a patented life-size one), Bibles in twenty languages, some six thousand styles of ornaments (together with "Merry Christmas" greeting ornaments in more than seventy languages), and 150 styles of nutcrackers.

Each year customers buy more than 1.3 million ornaments, over 700,000 feet of garland, nearly 100,000 postcards, and over 135,000 light sets (approximately 530 miles of light cords). The store displays more than 350 decorated Christmas trees and more than seven hundred animated figurines. Bronner's also boasts more than eight hundred different kinds of Hummel figurines and over one thousand different Precious Moments figurines.

More than two million guests visit Bronner's every year, and in December more than nine thousand children tell Santa Claus at Bronner's what they want for Christmas. In 1976, movie star John Wayne ordered a Santa suit from Bronner's by telephone. Celebrities who have sojourned to Bronner's include Olympic gold medalist Dorothy Hamill, singers Jim Nabors, Pat Boone, Marie Osmond, Andy Williams, the Lennon Sisters, the Lettermen, Ted Nugent, the Ink Spots, Faith Hill, Twila Paris, comedian Dave Coulier, Maria von Trapp, First Lady Laura Bush, and actress Cindy Williams. In fact, Bronner's has supplied Christmas decorations for the movies *Jingle All the Way, Enemy of the State, Must Be Santa, Simple Plan, Frost, Shaft, How the Grinch Stole Christmas, Riding in Cars with Boys, Serendipity, Call Me Claus, Catch Me If You Can, Analyze That,* and *Blizzard.*

Bronner's also sells Christmas displays to more than five thousand commercial and industrial accounts across the nation, including more than two thousand cities and one thousand shopping centers.

O, COME ALL YE HUNGRY

Kooky Christmas Cuisine

WHAT'S YOUR POISON?

In the nineteenth century, North Americans took the French drink Lait de Poule (a mixture of raw egg yolks, milk, and sugar) and added sherry, rum, and brandy, creating eggnog—a popular holiday beverage high in cholesterol and posing the threat of salmonella. Eggnog is now usually cooked to remove any possibility of food poisoning.

The Log 'n' Liver Special

The French serve bûche de Noël, a Christmas cake that looks like a miniature log. On Christmas Day, Parisians also eat oysters and pâté de foie gras (goose liver paste).

The Proof Is in the Pudding

The British insist that a wish made while mixing the traditional Christmas pudding will come true—but only if the ingredients are stirred in a clockwise direction.

It's Christmas Dinner! No, It's a Drain Cleaner!

On Christmas, Norwegians eat lutefisk (cod that has been soaked in lye, the main ingredient in Drāno).

Mmmmmmm! I Smell a Rat!

During the Prussian siege of France in 1870, Voisin's, an upscale restaurant in Paris, prepared a Christmas dinner using animals from the zoo and elsewhere. The menu included consommé of elephant, braised kangaroo, antelope pâté, cat, and rat.

Let's Talk Turkey

Did you ever wonder why eating turkey at Christmas dinner makes you feel tired? That's because turkey contains high amounts of tryptophan, an amino acid that induces fatigue.

Milk and Cookies? Bah, Humbug!

Australian children leave beer for Santa, British children leave out a sifter of brandy for Father Christmas, and children in the Tyrol leave out a glass of Schnapps for St. Nicholas.

for Santa

Gummy Worms

On Christmas, southern Africans eat plump, fuzzy caterpillars of the emperor moth (Gonimbrasia belina), fried in oil.

SOMETHING FISHY

On Christmas Eve, Italians dine on eel and squid.

A Slice of Christmas

In Japan, people celebrate Christmas Eve by ordering a Domino's pizza. Sales at Japanese Domino's franchises peak on December 24.

Cannibals in Training

For breakfast on Christmas morning, Belgians eat *cougnou*—a bread in the shape of the baby Jesus.

American Fruit Cakes

Americans serve aged fruit cakes made with nuts, raisins, and various fruits. When well-saturated with liquor and buried in powdered sugar in tightly closed tins, fruit cakes can be eaten up to twenty-five years after baking—perhaps explaining the phrase "nutty as a fruitcake" and giving birth to the saying "you are what you eat."

That Lascivious Pudding

Plum pudding originated in England during the Middle Ages as a thick porridge consisting of beef broth, tongue, fruit juice, wine, spices, and raisins. (The raisins swell up when cooked, giving the dish its name.) Thickened with eggs, bread crumbs, and dried fruit and flavored with ale and spirits, plum pudding was banned in 1664 as a "lewd custom" by the Puritans, who described the dessert's rich ingredients as "unfit for God-fearing people." In 1714, King George I, having tasted and enjoyed plum pudding, restored the dessert as part of the Christmas feast, despite objections by Quakers, who considered it "the invention of the scarlet whore of Babylon."

LET THEM EAT CRUMBS

At midnight on Christmas Eve, the Portuguese eat the *consoada*, a meal of fish and potato, setting extra places at the table for the spirits of the dead and scattering crumbs for them.

Man Cannot Live by Bread Alone

On the afternoon of January 6 (Epiphany), Mexican families share a traditional loaf of bread containing a doll of the baby Jesus.

The Rise of Gingerbread

In the eleventh century, Crusaders returned from the Middle East with ginger. European bakers began adding the new spice to breads, which became formally known as "gingerbread" in the fifteenth century. Laws enacted during the Protestant Reformation prohibited French and German gingerbread-makers from producing gingerbread at Christmas or Easter.

When Christmas markets *(Christkindlesmarkts)* sprang up throughout Germany in the sixteenth century, gingerbread bakers, who baked fresh gingerbread in their stalls, became a central attraction. The *Christkindlesmarkt* in Nuremberg, Germany, became known as the "gingerbread capital of the world"-famous for its gingerbread men and gingerbread houses decorated with candies, a German creation called *Hexenhaeusle.*

At the end of the nineteenth century, the fairy tale "Hansel and Gretel" by the Brothers Grimm popularized gingerbread houses. In the story, an unscrupulous witch lives in a gingerbread house to attract children that she cooks into gingerbread men in her oven. Hansel and Gretel escape after cleverly shoving the witch into her own oven.

THE CANDY CANE CONSPIRACY

Contrary to popular belief, the ubiquitous red-and-white-striped Christmas candy cane was not designed to incorporate any Christian religious symbolism.

As early as the mid-seventeenth century, Europeans decorated Christmas trees with cookies and candy, including white sticks of hard sugar candy.

Tradition holds that a German choirmaster at the Cologne Cathedral persuaded craftsmen to produce bent versions of the sugar sticks to represent a shepherd's staff, so he could pass them out to fidgety children attending the living Nativity (to keep them quiet).

Around 1847, German immigrant August Imgard of Wooster, Ohio, decorated his Christmas tree with white J-shaped candy canes to entertain his nephews and nieces. At the beginning of the twentieth century, candy makers added red stripes to candy canes.

Contemporary folklore retroactively assigned the candy canes the following religious symbolism:

- The white color suggests the Virgin Birth and the sinless nature of Jesus.
- The hardness of the candy represents Jesus as the rock of refuge.
- The J-shape signifies the name of Jesus and the staff of the "Good Shepherd."
- The three thin red stripes denote the Trinity or the stripes of the scourging Jesus received.
- The large red stripe symbolizes the blood shed by Jesus on the cross.
- The peppermint flavor is reminiscent of hyssop, associated with purification and sacrifice.

WEIRD
Tidings
Tinsel Town, Jingle Babies,
and the Odds of Having a White Christmas

The Christmas Price Index

Every year since 1984, PNC Advisors—the wealth management unit of the PNC Financial Services Group, Inc., one of the largest diversified financial services companies in the United States—has provided an economic analysis, based on the cost of goods and services purchased by the True Love in the Christmas carol "The Twelve Days of Christmas."

In 1984, all the receipts for "The Twelve Days of Christmas" totaled $12,623. Twenty years later, the total cost escalated to $17,297. "The Christmas Price Index," as PNC Advisors calls it, climbed an average of 1.6 percent every year for twenty years. In 2004, the high cost of fuel raised the cost of delivering a pear tree. Skilled labor, like the wages for the dancing ladies, increased an average of 5.5 percent every year for twenty years. The wages for the maids a-milking, however, rose an average of only 2.2 percent per year due to outsourcing of less skilled labor.

PNC Advisors calculated the total cost of all of the items in the famous carol, including the repetitions, at $66,334—up from $64,427.10 in 1984.

Fa La La La Huh? (The Weirdest Christmas Songs of All Time)

- *"Santa Claus Got Stuck in My Chimney"*—Ella Fitzgerald
- *"All I Want for Christmas Is a Beatle"* by Dora Bryan
- *"Christmas with the Devil"* by Spinal Tap
- *"The Twelve Days of Christmas"*—Bob and Doug McKenzie
- *"Green Chritma"*—Stan Freberg
- *"Chipmunk Song (Christmas Don't Be Late)"*—The Chipmunks
- *"All I Want for Christmas Is My Two Front Teeth"*— Spike Jones & His City Slickers
- *"I Want an Alien for Christmas"* by Fountains of Wayne
- *"[I'm Gettin'] Nuttin' for Christmas"*—Stan Freberg
- *"Christmas Carol"*—Tom Lehrer
- *"Grandma Got Run over by a Reindeer"*—Elmo & Patsy
- *"Jingle Bells"*—Singing Dogs
- *"The Twelve Gifts of Christmas"*—Allan Sherman
- *"I Want a Hippopotamus for Christmas"*—Gayla Peevey
- *"I'm a Christmas Tree"*— Wild Man Fischer
- *"I Saw Daddy Kissing Santa Claus"*—Kip Addotta
- *"Christmas at Ground Zero"*—Weird Al Yankovic

* 135 *

Hark, the Partridge Family Sings

The record album "A Partridge Family Christmas Card," released in 1972 at the height of the popularity of the television series *The Partridge Family*, includes eleven Christmas songs, but curiously excludes the song "The Twelve Days of Christmas," which features the familiar lyric, "And a partridge in a pear tree."

BARKING UP THE CHRISTMAS TREE

Recorded in 1955, the hit single record "Jingle Bells," by the Singing Dogs, features the sound of dogs barking the tune to the popular Christmas song. To record the song, producer Don Charles and director Carl Weismann spent hundreds of hours of recording barking dogs, putting the voices through a variable-speed oscillator to get the right pitches, and then painstakingly editing the sounds into a song that matches the rhythm with the backing track. The B-side of the original 45-rpm single features the dogs barking to "Oh Susanna."

Christmas Turkeys

Aside from making some classic Christmas movies, Hollywood has made some real turkeys:

- *Christmas Evil* (1983) A New York toy factory employee, traumatized by his child-hood memory of Santa cheating on Mrs. Claus with Mom, dresses as Santa Claus and cruises the streets in a van, dispensing toys and death.
- *Elves* (1990) Nazis try to coerce a young virgin working as a clerk in a Colorado department store to mate with a murderous elf on Christmas Eve and create a race of Aryan super-elves. After the elf kills a coke-snorting department store Santa, a homeless, ex-police detective (played by actor Dan Haggerty, who starred as television's Grizzly Adams) disguises himself as Santa to investigate.
- *A Jetson Christmas Carol* (1985) George Jetson lives his own spaced-out version of Charles Dickens's *A Christmas Carol,* with Mr. Spacely as his Scrooge-like boss.
- *Santa Claus Conquers the Martians* (1964) Four Martians—Bomar, Chechen, Dropo and Shim—kidnap Santa Claus and bring him to the Red Planet in the hopes of giving Mars some badly needed holiday spirit. But their plans go awry when the evil Voldar attempts to murder Santa in an airlock. This movie marks the screen debut of eight-year-old Pia Zadora.
- *Silent Night, Deadly Night* (1984) A young boy watches his parents get mur-dered by a lunatic in a Santa suit, and, after enduring several years of abuse in an orphanage, becomes a psychotic St. Nick who strangles a young tramp with a string of colorful Xmas lights. This horrid film inspired three sequels, including one featuring Mickey Rooney.
- *A Very Brady Christmas* (1988) This made-for-TV movie features Mrs. Brady lead-ing the town in a chorus of "O, Come All Ye Faithful" as she contemplates the fate of her husband Mike, who has been trapped under a collapsed construction site.

Holiday Film Goes Haywire
It's a (Weird and) Wonderful Life

★ Frank Capra's 1946 movie *It's a Wonderful Life,* although nominated for five Academy Awards, flopped at the box office. In the 1970s, after discovering that Liberty Films had failed to renew the movie's copyright, allowing the motion picture to fall into public domain, television stations began broadcasting it to their heart's content, popularizing the movie.

★ Bert and Ernie on Sesame Street were named after Bert the cop and Ernie the taxi driver in *It's a Wonderful Life.*

★ In the dinner scene before the high school graduation dance, Harry Bailey says, "Annie, my sweet, have you got those pies?" At that moment, the water pitcher on the table is about one-third full. Later in the scene, the pitcher has miraculously filled halfway with water.

★ During the courtship scene, George Bailey and his childhood sweetheart Mary Hatch dance in the Bedford Hills High School gymnasium. A jealous rival named Freddie (played by Carl Switzer, who starred as Alfalfa in the *Little Rascals* comedies) pushes a button, which causes the gymnasium floor to slide open, revealing a swimming pool that everyone falls into. The scene, filmed at Beverly Hills High School, features the "Swim/Gym," still in operation just south of the main school building, next to the school's sports field.

★ While walking home from the graduation dance, Mary accidentally loses her bathrobe and jumps into a nearby bush to hide. She tells George that she's hiding in a hydrangea bush, but the plant looks nothing like a hydrangea. When George tosses the robe onto the bush, it immediately vanishes.

★ When George walks into the Building and Loan carrying a Christmas wreath, the wreath disappears and reappears from his arm.

★ When George crashes his car into a tree, the car has no snow on it. In the subsequent shot, snowdrifts cover the car.

★ When George tells Clarence, "I wish I'd never been born," Clarence stands with his arms at his side. In the next shot, Clarence's arms are suddenly crossed.

Bah, Humbug

Charles Dickens, author of *A Christmas Carol* (1843), one of the most famous stories ever written, suffered a desperately poor childhood, working in a London factory pasting labels on bottles of shoe polish.

Snow Job

Chris Van Allsburg, a convert to Judaism, wrote and illustrated the children's book, The Polar Express.

Here Comes Santa Claus ...Ooops

In the 1984 film *Gremlins*, Kate Beringer (played by Phoebe Cates) tells her friend Zach Galligan that when she was a child her father disappeared before Christmas and was found several days later, stuck halfway down the chimney with a bag of toys.

JINGLE BABIES

The Jingle Babies, a chorus of twenty-seven infants ranging in age from two weeks to two years, provide vocals for twelve Christmas songs on the album *Rockabye Christmas*. In 1997, producer Mike Spalla recorded 500 different baby sounds—burps, coos, cries, giggles, hiccoughs, and sighs—and then edited them together over a music bed peppered with the sounds of rattles and toy squeaks. The album includes such all-time favorites as "Silent Night," "Jingle Bells," "O Christmas Tree," "What Child Is This?," "Carol of the Bells," and "Dance of the Sugarplum Fairies."

This wasn't the first time Spalla had immersed himself in such a time-intensive recording project. His obsession with unusual sounds began in 1993. Inspired by a 1955 recording of dogs singing "Jingle Bells," Spalla recorded more than a thousand sounds made by several cats he rescued and named the Jingle Cats, slowing down or speeding up their purrs and meows to follow the melodies of several Christmas songs. He spliced together enough songs to fill an album called "Meowy Christmas," which includes the songs "Silent Night," "Oh, Come All Ye Faithful," and "Deck the Halls." The album reached Number 10 on the Billboard Charts. In 1994, Spalla followed up with a second Jingle Cats album of caterwauling called "Here Comes Santa Claws," which featured the songs "O, Holy Night," "The Little Drummer Boy," and "Ave Maria." In 1995, he decided to take the original concept of the barking dogs a step further and recorded the Jingle Dogs album "Christmas Unleashed." The Jingle Dogs bark out such classic Christmas favorites as " We Wish You a Merry Christmas," "O Christmas Tree," and "Away in a Manger."

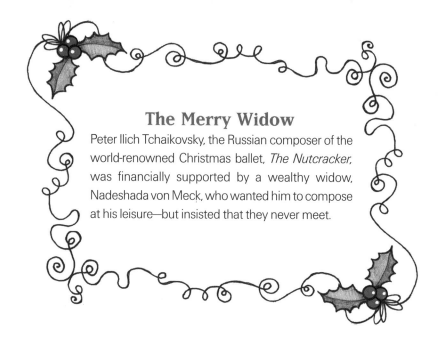

The Merry Widow

Peter Ilich Tchaikovsky, the Russian composer of the world-renowned Christmas ballet, *The Nutcracker,* was financially supported by a wealthy widow, Nadeshada von Meck, who wanted him to compose at his leisure—but insisted that they never meet.

HAVE A KUNG FU CHRISTMAS

On December 21, 1974, the half-hour long *National Lampoon Radio Hour Show,* broadcast "Kung Fu Christmas," a Motown parody that mocked the hit song "Everybody Was Kung Fu Fighting." The song, written and sung by Brian Doyle Murray, Bill Murray, and Gilda Radner (to music by Paul Shaffer and Christopher Guest), includes the lyrics:

> "Santa Claus makin' the Soul Train scene,
> Slickin' down his beard with Afro-Sheen.
> Eenie meenie and minie moes,
> Frost in the air and snow up your nose."

Good Grief!

In 1965, CBS Network executives almost cancelled the premier of the animated television special, "A Charlie Brown Christmas."

Producer Lee Mendelson, animator Bill Melendez, and Peanuts creator Charles Schulz presented the finished show to CBS network executives just ten days before the scheduled airdate. Unfortunately, the network executives hated it. They objected to the shoddy animation, the slow pace, the religious content (Charlie Brown complains about the overcommercialization of Christmas, and Linus quotes from the Gospel of Luke), the incongruous choice of a jazz score, the lack of a laugh track, and the use of genuine children as the voiceover talent.

Mendelson and Schulz agreed that the animation was second-rate. The rushed animation production created several continuity mistakes: Schroeder lifts his fingers from the piano keys while the music continues to play, Pig Pen disappears from the screen momentarily in the middle of a song, and the barren Christmas tree loses some branches which inexplicably reappear. The production was so rushed that Mendelson wrote the lyrics for the song "Christmas Time Is Here" on an envelope in roughly fifteen minutes.

With only ten days to go before the airdate, CBS executives had no alternative but to the air the special as scheduled on December 9, 1965. Despite the network's criticisms, 15 million homes tuned in to watch "A Charlie Brown Christmas," making the special that week's second-highest-rated show (after *Bonanza*). The show, winning both an Emmy and Peabody Award, became the longest-running animated annual special in television history. Ironically, even before "A Charlie Brown Christmas" aired on television, Peanuts had generated heavy merchandise sales, making Charlie Brown's complaint about Christmas commercialism seem somewhat paradoxical.

★ Eight of the top ten Christmas songs of all time where written by Jews.

★ A Jew wrote the most popular Christmas song ever. "(I'm Dreaming of a) White Christmas," written by Irving Berlin for the movie *Holiday Inn* (1942) and sung by Bing Crosby, is the best-selling record of all time. Irving Berlin was born Israel Isidore Baline on May 11, 1888, in Siberia. He immigrated to New York's Lower East Side with his family at the age of five. His father was a part-time cantor in a synagogue. Berlin also wrote the hit song "Easter Parade" and received the Congressional Gold Medal for his song "God Bless America." Although he wrote nearly one thousand songs, he could only play and compose on the piano in the key of F sharp. The 1954 movie *White Christmas*, a film about song-and-dance men who romance women during the holidays in a Vermont ski lodge, features a Jewish star (Danny Kaye, born David Kaminsky), a Jewish director (Michael Curtiz), a Jewish screenwriter (Norman Krasna), and a Jewish composer (Irving Berlin). The song "White Christmas" has been recorded by the Beach Boys, Bob Dylan, and Bob Marley, among countless others.

★ J. Fred Coots, who wrote the music to the second-most-performed Christmas song of all time, "Santa Claus is Coming to Town," was Jewish. Singer and entertainer Eddie Cantor, born on New York's Lower East Side to Russian-Jewish immigrant parents, introduced the song on his radio show in 1934.

★ Mel Torme, the son of Russian-Jewish immigrants, wrote the third-most-performed Christmas tune, "The Christmas Song" (Chestnuts Roasting on an Open Fire), in less than an hour. Nat King Cole recorded the song in 1945.

★ Mitchell Parish, co-writer of the sixth-most-performed Christmas song, "Sleigh Ride," was a Jewish immigrant to the United States from Lithuania and is buried in Beth David Cemetery in Elmont, New York.

★ Jewish composer Jerry Herman, who wrote the music and lyrics for three of the longest running musicals in Broadway history, *Hello Dolly!*, *Mame*, and *La Cage aux Folles*, wrote the song "We Need a Little Christmas" for *Mame*. Angela Lansbury first sang the song on Broadway in 1966.

- Johnny Marks, who wrote the hit songs "Rudolph the Red-Nosed Reindeer," "Rockin' Around the Christmas Tree," and "A Holly Jolly Christmas" was Jewish.
- Lyricist Sammy Cahn (born Samuel Cohen) and songwriter Jule Styne (born Julius Kerwin Stein), who wrote "The Christmas Waltz" and "Let It Snow, Let It Snow, Let It Snow," were both Jewish.
- Jewish songwriting team Ray Evans and Jay Livingston wrote the popular Christmas song, "Silver Bells." Together, three-time Academy Award–winners Livingston and Evans also wrote the hit songs "Mona Lisa," "Que Sera, Sera," and the classic television themes for *Bonanza* and *Mr. Ed*.
- Jewish composer Albert Hague wrote the song "You're a Mean One, Mr. Grinch" for the 1966 animated television special "How the Grinch Stole Christmas." Hague, who escaped Nazi Germany at the age of eighteen, won a Tony Award for his score of the Broadway musical *Redhead* and starred as Professor Shorofsky, the music teacher in the film and television series *Fame*.
- In the nineteenth century, French-Jewish composer Adolphe Adam wrote the music for "O Holy Night." Lyricist Placide Cappeau, of the village of Roquemaure, repudiated Christianity and embraced free thought late in life.
- The Christmas carol "Hark the Herald Angels Sing" by Charles Wesley, brother of John Wesley who founded the Methodist church, was written in 1739 as "Hark, How All the Welkin Rings," and sung to slow and solemn music. More than a hundred years later, in 1840, Jewish composer Felix Mendelssohn wrote a cantata to commemorate Johannes Gutenberg's invention of the printing press. In 1855, three years after the death of Mendelssohn, English musician William Cummings changed the first line of Wesley's lyrics from "Hark, how all the welkin rings" to "Hark the herald angels sing" and adapted Mendelssohn's music to fit the lyrics—despite evidence that neither Wesley nor Mendelssohn would have approved.
- Famous Jewish entertainers who have recorded Christmas albums include Barry Manilow, Kenny G, Barbra Streisand, Neil Diamond, Herb Alpert, Phil Spector, Michael Bolton, and Harry Connick, Jr.

How the Grinch Stole Christmas

In 1957, Theodore Geisel, the author and illustrator of dozens of highly imaginative children's books published under the pseudonym Dr. Seuss, produced *How the Grinch Stole Christmas*. The cranky old Grinch, sickened by the overabundance of Christmas cheer teeming from the happy village of Whoville, decides to hijack the holiday by masquerading as Santa Claus and disguising his dog Max as a reindeer—but he ultimately succumbs to the joys of the season.

Nine years later, Dr. Seuss turned the book into an animated television special by teaming up with a talented animator with whom he had previously collaborated on a series of military training films during World War II. That animator was Chuck Jones, the creator of Bugs Bunny, Daffy Duck, the Roadrunner, Wile E. Coyote, and Pepé Le Pew.

Actor Boris Karloff, who starred as the Frankenstein monster and the Mummy in movies, provided the voice of both the Grinch and the story's narrator. Songwriter Albert Hague wrote the songs, including "You're a Mean One, Mister Grinch," sung by Thurl Ravenscroft, the voice of Tony the Tiger on commercials for Kellogg's Frosted Flakes.

In 2000, Universal Studios released the movie version of *How the Grinch Stole Christmas*, directed by Ron Howard and starring Jim Carrey as the Grinch. When asked if he had ever worked on a project as big and expensive as this, actor Jeffery Tambor, who co-starred as Mayor Maywho, replied, "Maybe my bar mitzvah."

A bronze statue of the Grinch and his dog Max are immortalized at the Dr. Seuss National Memorial Sculpture Garden at the Springfield Museums in Springfield, Massachusetts.

The Whoville Connection

In *How the Grinch Stole Christmas*, the Grinch attempts to steal Christmas from the Whos, unusual creatures who live in Whoville. But the Grinch isn't the only Dr. Seuss character who encounters the Whos of Whoville. In the Dr. Seuss book *Horton Hears a Who!*, published three years before *How the Grinch Stole Christmas*,

The Official
Ebenezer Scrooge
Humbug Count

Movie	Year	Star	Number of Humbugs
Scrooge	1935	Sir Seymour Hicks	5
A Christmas Carol	1938	Reginald Owen	10
A Christmas Carol	1951	Alastair Sim	5
Scrooge	1970	Albert Finney	6
Mickey's Christmas Carol	1983	Scrooge McDuck	5
Scrooged	1988	Bill Murray	2

Horton the Elephant saves the tiny Whos of Whoville, microscopic creatures who live on a small particle of dust that happens to be blowing through the air toward a watery fate. If the Grinch and Horton tangled with the same Whos in the same Whoville, then the Grinch is infinitesimally small.

Goodwill Toward Men?

Some Christmas carols seem to advocate tolerance toward homosexuality. The lyrics to "Deck the Halls" encourage celebrants to don "gay apparel," and the holiday song "Have Yourself a Merry Little Christmas" urges people to "Make the Yuletide gay."

I'll Be Jailed for Christmas

O. Henry, author of the classic Christmas story "The Gift of the Magi," spent three years in prison for embezzlement.

SANTA CLAUS IS COMING TO BEDROCK

In Episode 130 of the animated television series *The Flintstones* ("Christmas Flintstones"), Fred takes a job as a department store Santa Claus and winds up substituting for the real Santa Claus when he gets sick—despite the fact that the Flintstones takes place in the Stone Age (approximately 1 million years before the birth of Jesus).

Beat It, Kid

In the Christmas song, "The Little Drummer Boy," a poor shepherd, unable to afford a gift for the baby Jesus, chooses to play a song on his drum for the infant in the manger. In reality, Mother Mary might not have considered a young boy's drumming for a newborn baby a very welcome gift.

KAZOO CHRISTMAS

Kazoo Christmas contains a collection of favorite Christmas songs performed by the Kickin Kazoos, a group of kazoo players from around the world. The CD comes with a red and green plastic Kazoo so you can play along.

Do They Know It's Christmas?

In 1984, several pop and rock stars—including Bob Geldof, Phil Collins, Bono, Sting, George Michael, and Boy George—joined together as "Band-Aid" and recorded a song to raise money to buy food and medical supplies for the victims of a widespread famine in Ethiopia. The resulting song, "Do They Know It's Christmas?" written by Bob Geldof and Midge Ure, sold more than 3 million copies. Critics pointed out that the majority of people in Ethiopia are Moslems and animists and do not celebrate Christmas, so the answer to the question posed in the song title would be that roughly 35 percent of the people in Ethiopia know it's Christmas.

A DYSFUNCTIONAL FAMILY CHRISTMAS

If you're anticipating a dysfunctional family Christmas dinner, why not play disturbing music to darken the mood even further? A CD titled *A Dysfunctional Family Christmas*, and aptly subtitled "Music for your Misery," contains a selection of grim classics like Richard Wagner's "Siegfried's Funeral March," Modest Petrovich Mussorgsky's "Night on Bald Mountain," and Gustav Holst's "Mars, the Bringer of War."

Let's Kill Gary Gilmore for Christmas

In 1976, convicted murderer Gary Gilmore requested that his death sentence be carried out by firing squad. In response to his request, people inundated prison officials with phone calls volunteering to shoot Gilmore, the media called for a public execution, all three major television networks requested permission to televise the event, and Gilmore's lawyer began negotiating with publishers and motion picture studios for book and movie rights.

On December 11, 1976, toward the end of the weekly broadcast of *Saturday Night Live*, guest host Candice Bergen announced that in the spirit of this national outcry, the cast of the show had prepared a very special Christmas song. As fake snow fell from above, cast members Gilda Radner, Dan Aykroyd, Jane Curtin, John Belushi, Laraine Newman, and Garrett Morris debuted the lilting Christmas song, "Let's Kill Gary Gilmore for Christmas." Despite public outrage over the song, the show won an Emmy Award.

Klezmer Christmas Carols

Oy to the World: A Klezmer Christmas, a CD of classic Christmas carols performed in the musical style of Eastern European Jewish villages, or *shtetls*, has attracted a cult following among interfaith couples. Produced by advertising jingle producer Paul Libman and his band the Klezmonauts (including renowned Chicago musicians Johnny Frigo, Fareed Haque, Arnie Roth, and Bobby Lewis), this quirky melding of Santa Claus and *Fiddler on the Roof* offers hilarious and deeply moving versions of "Deck the Halls," "Away in the Manger," and an original Yiddish song titled "Santa Gey Gezhunderheit."

LET IT SNOW

Dreaming of a white Christmas? According to weather records provided by the National Climatic Data Center and averaged over a thirty-year period, here are your chances of having at least the amount of snow at the top of each column on the ground on Christmas Day in the largest American cities:

City	Chances of At Least		
	1"	5"	10"
Albuquerque, New Mexico	3%	0%	0%
Anchorage, Alaska	90%	70%	37%
Atlanta, Georgia	0%	0%	0%
Billings, Montana	63%	17%	0%
Birmingham, Alabama	0%	0%	0%
Boise, Idaho	30%	10%	0%
Boston, Massachusetts	23%	17%	3%
Burlington, Vermont	77%	50%	13%
Casper, Wyoming	47%	10%	3%
Charleston, West Virginia	30%	3%	0%
Charlotte, North Carolina	0%	0%	0%
Chicago, Illinois	40%	7%	0%
Cincinnati, Ohio	11%	4%	0%
Cleveland, Ohio	50%	17%	0%
Columbia, South Carolina	0%	0%	0%
Columbus, Ohio	23%	0%	0%
Concord, New Hampshire	87%	57%	7%
Dallas, Texas	0%	0%	0%
Denver, Colorado	50%	13%	7%
Des Moines, Iowa	50%	17%	7%
Detroit, Michigan	50%	13%	0%
El Paso, Texas	0%	0%	0%
Fairbanks, Alaska	100%	100%	77%
Fresno, California	0%	0%	0%
Grand Forks, North Dakota	89%	46%	7%
Hartford, Connecticut	57%	23%	3%
Honolulu, Hawaii	0%	0%	0%

Houston, Texas	0%	0%	0%
Indianapolis, Indiana	30%	3%	0%
Jackson, Mississippi	0%	0%	0%
Jacksonville, Florida	0%	0%	0%
Las Vegas, Nevada	0%	0%	0%
Little Rock, Arkansas	3%	0%	0%
Los Angeles, California	0%	0%	0%
Louisville, Kentucky	13%	0%	0%
Memphis, Tennessee	7%	3%	3%
Miami, Florida	0%	0%	0%
Milwaukee, Wisconsin	60%	10%	3%
Minneapolis, Minnesota	73%	30%	13%
Nashville, Tennessee	13%	3%	0%
New York, New York	10%	7%	0%
New Orleans, Louisiana	0%	0%	0%
Newark, New Jersey	23%	10%	0%
Oklahoma City, Oklahoma	3%	0%	0%
Omaha, Nebraska	44%	8%	4%
Philadelphia, Pennsylvania	10%	7%	3%
Phoenix, Arizona	0%	0%	0%
Pittsburgh, Pennsylvania	33%	7%	0%
Portland, Oregon	83%	43%	13%
Portland, Oregon	0%	0%	0%
Providence, Rhode Island	37%	10%	0%
Sacramento, California	0%	0%	0%
Salisbury, Maryland	14%	3%	0%
Salt Lake City, Utah	53%	13%	3%
San Francisco, California	0%	0%	0%
San Antonio, Texas	0%	0%	0%
San Diego, California	0%	0%	0%
Seattle, Washington	7%	0%	0%
Sioux Falls, South Dakota	67%	27%	7%
St. Louis, Missouri	23%	3%	0%
Toledo, Ohio	57%	3%	0%
Tucson, Arizona	3%	0%	0%
Tulsa, Oklahoma	7%	0%	0%
Virginia Beach, Virginia	0%	0%	0%
Washington, D.C.	13%	7%	0%
Wichita, Kansas	23%	0%	0%
Wilmington, Delaware	13%	3%	3%

Melt in Your Mouth, Not in Your Christmas Stocking

In the 1980s, the M&M Mars Company launched a special holiday line of red and green M&M's Chocolate Candies for Christmas. Ironically, red and green are the most controversial M&M's colors.

In 1976, after scientists determined that Red Dye Number 2 caused cancer in rats, M&M's Chocolate Candies stopped making red M&M's (which did not contain Red Dye Number 2) and replaced them with tan M&M's, sparking protests from the Society for the Restoration and Preservation of Red M&M's. In 1987, the company brought back red M&M's, using FD&C Red Number 40.

Green M&M's are considered to be an aphrodisiac. At wedding showers, guests often present the future bride with a bag of M&M's with all the green candies carefully removed and placed in a second bag specifically reserved for the wedding night. An M&M Mars brochure states: "Although many consumers ask us about the special qualities of green M&M's Chocolate Candies, we cannot explain any extraordinary 'powers' attributed to this color, either scientifically or medically."

NEW AND IMPROVED KISSES UNDER THE MISTLETOE

In 1962, Hershey's introduced Hershey's Kisses wrapped in red and green foil for the Christmas season.

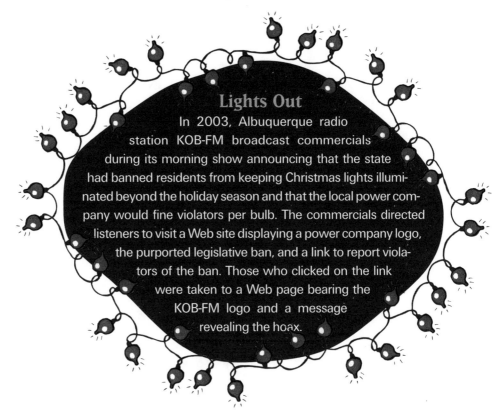

Lights Out

In 2003, Albuquerque radio station KOB-FM broadcast commercials during its morning show announcing that the state had banned residents from keeping Christmas lights illuminated beyond the holiday season and that the local power company would fine violators per bulb. The commercials directed listeners to visit a Web site displaying a power company logo, the purported legislative ban, and a link to report violators of the ban. Those who clicked on the link were taken to a Web page bearing the KOB-FM logo and a message revealing the hoax.

Crackers for Christmas

For Christmas in 1902, the National Biscuit Company (which eventually became known as Nabisco) redesigned its box of animal crackers, renamed "Barnum's Animals" in honor of renowned circus showman P. T. Barnum, as a circus wagon cage with a string handle so the box could be hung as a Christmas tree ornament. Barnum's Animals, selling for five cents a box, were an instant hit and immediately became a year-round favorite.

PLENTY OF ROOM AT THE INN

In 2004, a branch of the Travelodge hotel chain in London's Covent Garden offered any couple with the first names Mary and Joseph a free night's stay on Christmas Eve. "We are trying to make up for the hotel industry not having any rooms left on Christmas Eve 2,004 years ago," said hotel manager Sandy Leckie. To take advantage of the offer, eligible couples—unlike the original Mary and Joseph—had to show legal identification.

The Genuine Article

In 1968, Miles Kimball, a mail-order firm based in Oshkosh, Wisconsin, featured Oshkosh B'Gosh children's overalls—then manufactured solely as a novelty item —in its national Christmas catalog. At the time, Oshkosh B'Gosh primarily sold rugged overalls for adult Midwestern farmers and railroad workers. Thanks to the catalog, Oshkosh B'Gosh was inundated with nearly fifteen thousand orders for children's overalls—accidentally propelling Oshkosh B'Gosh into the children's wear market. By 1993, children's clothing represented 95 percent of Oshkosh B'Gosh sales.

The Wal-Mart That Stole Christmas?

In early December 2002, the manager of the Wal-Mart in Sterling, Colorado, returned all the donated items in a Toys for Tots drop box to store shelves to be resold.

Store manager Brad Barritt claimed that he told Susan Kraich, the organizer of the annual Toys for Tots drive for the Logan County Chamber of Commerce, that all donated toys had to be wrapped in Wal-Mart bags to ensure that shoppers had not taken toys from the shelves and placed them in the box without paying for them. Kraich insisted that Barritt never communicated those instructions to her, and no one posted those instructions over the Toys for Tots donation box, which Wal-Mart foolishly placed in a spot out of range of any security cameras.

Barritt said that Wal-Mart would replace any item that Kraich could prove had been in the drop box. Kraich had receipts for only three toys—the ones she had purchased and put in the drop box herself.

After a wave of bad publicity in the media and irate phone calls, Wal-Mart's National Headquarters delivered $425 worth of toys to Kraich's office to make amends for the unfortunate incident.

WEIRD
Festivities
Christmas Sleighings, Lady Santas, and Kicking the Yuletide Bucket

Jolly Good?

In England, the rarely enforced "Holy Days and Fasting Days Act of 1551" requires all people to walk to church on Christmas Day and attend services. Under the act, any vehicle driven to church on Christmas Day may be confiscated by the police and sold to benefit the poor. Similarly, the "Unlawful Games Act of 1541" bans all sports except archery on Christmas Day (ancillary laws permit leaping and vaulting). In 1646, the Long Parliament outlawed eating a Christmas dinner with more than three courses and banned the eating of mince pies and Christmas pudding, describing both dishes as "abominable and idolatrous." The laws remain on the books.

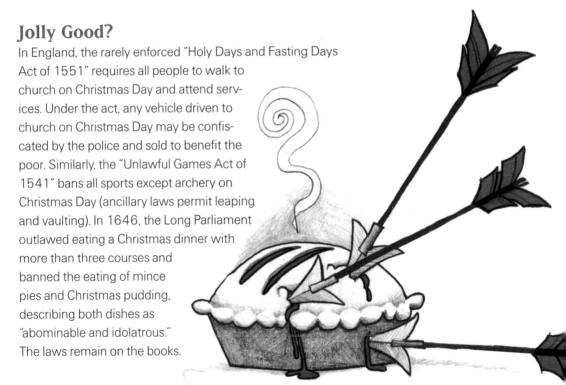

Christmas Cake

In 2004, Julie West of Edmonds, Washington, decided to protest against the increasing secularization of Christmas. She sent a cake to a holiday party at her son's first-grade class. The red icing spelled out "Happy Birthday Jesus."

INSTRUMENTAL CHRISTMAS

In 2004 in Maplewood, New Jersey, parents and students petitioned the local school board after school officials at Columbia High School banned the brass ensemble from playing an instrumental version of "Santa Claus Is Coming to Town."

WHAT'S THE POINT?

In Minnesota, in December 2001, Ramsey County manager Paul Kirkwold banned the traditional display of red poinsettias (symbolizing Christmas) from the courthouse in St. Paul, and instead decorated the courthouse with ribbons (representing flags from around the world). St. Paul's Jewish mayor, Norm Coleman, condemned the ban and demanded that the poinsettias be returned to the courthouse. The ensuing compromise? White poinsettias (representing nothing in particular).

Is Christmas Constitutional?

The First Amendment to the Constitution of the United States guarantees that "Congress shall make no law respecting an establishment of religion, or prohibiting the free exercise thereof . . ." In other words, this amendment forbids Congress to set up and in any way provide for an established church. Many courts have interpreted the First Amendment to mean that the government may not promote or give special treatment to any religion.

Christmas has not always been a national holiday in the United States. In 1836, sixty years after the founding of the country, Alabama became the first state to declare Christmas a legal holiday, followed by Louisiana and Arkansas in 1838. By 1856, every state in the union had made Christmas a legal holiday. On June 26, 1870, under the presidential leadership of Ulysses S. Grant, Congress declared Christmas a national holiday. In September 1966, Congress enacted United States Code (5 USC 6103), making Christmas the only religious holiday in America recognized as a national legal public holiday, closing down most government offices and services.

In 1998, Cincinnati attorney Richard Ganulin filed a lawsuit in U.S. District Court against the United States, asserting that the establishment of Christmas as a legal holiday violates the separation of church and state. "If we're going to be fair and uphold the constitution," Ganulin said, "we should realize that Christmas is a religious holiday, that it commemorates a religious event, and that it has religious origins."

The establishment of Christmas as a legal holiday, Ganulin argued, "unfairly interferes with [his] natural and equal freedom of belief, makes it more difficult to live in a way consistent with [his] own beliefs, obstructs [his] ability to teach [his] children, makes it less likely they will understand and respect [his] beliefs, negates [his] essential identity, imposes outsider political status, and directly leads to the unlawful expenditure of taxpayer funds by providing a specific government-imposed paid holiday for federal employees on a day of Christian celebration."

In 1999, U.S. District Judge Susan J. Dlott dismissed the suit by reciting a nine-stanza poem she had penned in the whimsical style of Dr. Seuss, author of *How the Grinch Stole Christmas*. The judge ruled that Christmas "has a valid secular purpose, it does not have the effect of endorsing religion in general or Christianity in particular, and it does not impermissibly cause excessive entanglement between church and state."

In 2000, Ganulin appealed the case before the Sixth U.S. Circuit Court of Appeals in Cincinnati, Ohio, at a time when the movie *The Grinch* was the #1 box office hit at movie theaters across the country. After hearing oral arguments, the court summarily affirmed Judge Dlott's opinion.

Ganulin appealed to the United States Supreme Court, which has never ruled on the constitutionality of the Christmas holiday. However, in a 1984 Supreme Court case concerning an official display of the Christian Nativity scene in Pawtucket, Rhode Island, Justice Sandra Day O'Connor acknowledged that governmental endorsement of Christmas "sends a message to non-adherents that they are outsiders, not full members of the political community, and an accompanying message to adherents that they are insiders, favored members of the political community."

Yet, on April 16, 2001, the U.S. Supreme Court refused to hear Ganulin's case, allowing Judge Dlotto's ruling to stand.

Christmas Ruling
By Judge Susan Dlott

The court will address
    Plaintiff's seasonal confusion,
Erroneously believing Christmas
    merely a religious intrusion.
Whatever the reason
    Constitutional or other,
Christmas is not an act of Big
    Brother!
Christmas is about joy and giving
    and sharing.
It is about the child within us.
It is mostly about caring!

One is never jailed for
  not having a tree,
For not going to church,
  for not spreading glee!
The court will uphold seemingly
  contradictory causes,
Decreeing "The Establishment"[1] and
  "Santa" both worthwhile "Claus(es)!"
We are all better for Santa,
  the Easter Bunny too,
And maybe the Great Pumpkin
  to name just a few!

An extra day off
  is hardly high treason.
It may be spent as you wish
  regardless of reason.
The court having read
  the lessons of "Lynch"[2]
Refuses to play the role of the
  Grinch!
There is room in this country
  and in all our hearts too
For different convictions
  and a day off too!

[1] The establishment of religion clause of the First Amendment.
[2] A 1984 U.S. Supreme Court decision.

Decriminalizing Christmas

In the 1500s, the Puritans—members of a religious movement determined to "purify" the Church of England—stopped celebrating Christmas with joyous "heathen traditions," which they considered to be "pagan mockery" of a sacred event. The majority of pilgrims sailing to the New World in 1620 aboard the *Mayflower* were Puritans eager to escape the jurisdiction of the Church of England, which they believed violated biblical precepts. The Pilgrims founded Plymouth Colony in Massachusetts, and the following November, thirty-five new settlers, unfamiliar with the Puritans' strict religious codes, arrived aboard the British ship *Fortune*. On Christmas Day in 1621, Governor William Bradford was appalled to find the new settlers playing traditional winter solstice games, such as "stoole bar" and "pitching the barr." He confiscated the gaming equipment, reprimanded the new settlers, and labeled their behavior sacrilegious.

When Puritan leader Oliver Cromwell came to power in England in 1649, the government banned Christmas celebrations, and soldiers tore down seasonal decorations and imposed penalties on people who celebrated Christmas or stayed home from work on Christmas Day. The prohibition spread to North America, where, in 1651, the Massachusetts General Court ordered that any person found "observing any such day as Christmas" be fined five shillings. In 1660, King Charles II, having been restored to the throne, lifted the ban on Christmas. In America, the influx of German and Irish immigrants in the nineteenth century infused the holiday with increased cheer, and finally, in 1856, Massachusetts declared Christmas a legal holiday.

GREETINGS

Forty-four percent of those Americans surveyed said the trend toward wishing people "Happy Holidays" rather than "Merry Christmas" is a change for the better, according to a CNN/USA Today/Gallup Poll conducted in December 2004. Forty-three percent disagreed.

Blue Christmas

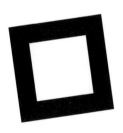

The notion that more people commit suicide on Christmas than on any other day of the year is a myth. In the United States, several studies have shown that there is no significant rise in suicide rates at Christmas. In fact, the average number of daily suicides drops in the month of December—which seems to indicate that the Christmas season gives suicidal people the will to live (at least until the credit card bill arrives in January).

You Can't Spell Christmas
Without Christ
(Unless You're an Incredibly Bad Speller)

Every year during the holiday season, Nativity scenes are erected on public property, and a lawsuit quickly follows to remove these government-sponsored religious messages because they violate the strict separation between church and state.

Why all the hullabaloo?

In the words of Supreme Court Justice Sandra Day O'Connor, religious displays on public property "send a message to non-adherents that they are outsiders, not full members of the political community, and an accompanying message to adherents that they are insiders, favored members of the political community."

But the Supreme Court has yet to clearly define whether a religious display sends a message of religious endorsement. Instead, the Court rules on a case-by-case basis to determine whether local government officials have sufficiently "secularized" their manger scene by adding enough figures of Frosty the Snowman and Santa Claus.

It all started in 1984, when the Supreme Court ruled in the case *Lynch v. Donnelly* that a city-sponsored Nativity scene in a public park does not violate the First Amendment if the Nativity scene also includes "secular" symbols of the holiday, such as a Christmas tree, a Santa Claus house, and cut-out figures of a clown, a dancing elephant, a robot, and a teddy bear. (Curiously, the court determined that a Christmas tree and Santa Claus are secular symbols—despite their religious origins.)

In 1989, the Supreme Court ruled in the case *Allegheny County v. ACLU* that a privately owned Nativity scene on the main staircase of a county courthouse does violate the First Amendment if it is not accompanied by Santa or dancing elephants, which were displayed elsewhere in the courthouse. The Judges also ruled that a nearby display, featuring an 18-foot-tall Hanukkah menorah placed next to a 45-foot-tall Christmas tree, did not violate the First Amendment (because the secular meaning of the menorah somehow offset the religious symbolism of the tree).

Every since those two decisions, the Supreme Court has been hearing case after case, essentially counting candy canes to determine if Nativity scenes have been secularized enough—as if the addition of Rudolph the Red-Nosed Reindeer diminishes the religious significance of the baby Jesus in a manager.

The result? Overly cautious local governments and school officials have banned Nativity scenes and Christmas trees from public property, prohibited the mention of Jesus during Christmas celebrations, and forbidden the use of the word "Christmas" in public parades, schools, and celebrations. Some schools have dropped Christmas carols from holiday programs. (Court decisions do permit public school students to study religion and to perform religious music as part of the curriculum, provided that religious practices are not endorsed.)

Christians and traditionalists across the nation, incensed by attempts to downplay the religious significance of Christmas, have filed lawsuits, promoted boycotts, and launched campaigns aimed at restoring references to Jesus in seasonal celebrations.

Skeptics joke that the Supreme Court has ruled that there cannot be a Nativity scene in Washington, DC, because they have been unable to find three wise men and a virgin in the nation's capitol. There has never been any problem, they add, finding enough asses to fill the stable.

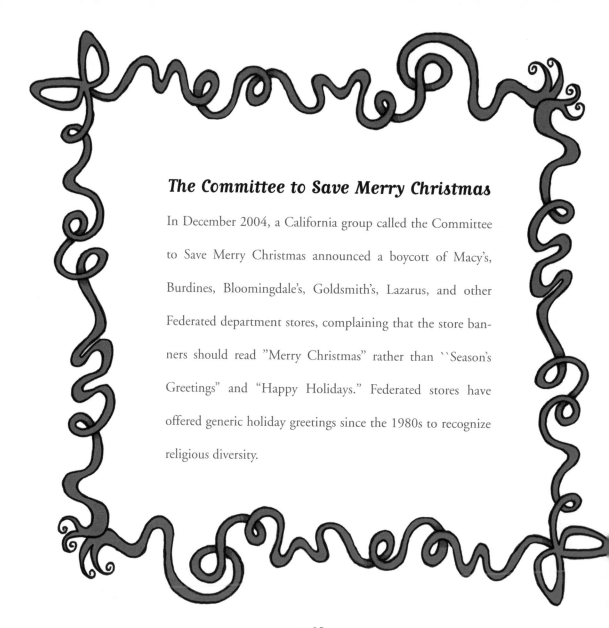

The Committee to Save Merry Christmas

In December 2004, a California group called the Committee to Save Merry Christmas announced a boycott of Macy's, Burdines, Bloomingdale's, Goldsmith's, Lazarus, and other Federated department stores, complaining that the store banners should read "Merry Christmas" rather than ``Season's Greetings" and "Happy Holidays." Federated stores have offered generic holiday greetings since the 1980s to recognize religious diversity.

Jesus vs. Quetzalcoatl

In November 1994, officials in San Jose, California, ordered the city to remove a privately funded Nativity scene from the city's annual Christmas display in the park to avoid offending the city's non-Christian citizens. But two weeks earlier in that same park, those same city officials unveiled a permanent eight-foot-tall statue of Quetzalcoatl, the feathered serpent-god of ancient Mesoamerica—ignoring protests from offended Christians. Built at a cost of $500,000 with public funds, the statue was meant to be a multicultural symbol in honor of San Jose's Latino community. A federal district court ruled that erecting pagan idols with tax dollars does not violate the separation between church and state if people no longer worship the idol. Ultimately, after 2,000 residents swarmed city hall to protest the removal of the Nativity scene, San Jose officials agreed to return Joseph, Mary, and the baby Jesus to the park.

Bloody Jesus

A gory parade float featured a young man portraying the crucified Jesus in the 1994 Lights Fantastic Parade in Carbondale, Illinois. The young man, clad in a loincloth and a crown of thorns, wore bloody makeup all over his face and body, and hung from a cross. The resulting flood of complaints prompted parade organizers to ban the church that sponsored the bloody float from participating in future parades.

Causeway Commotion

In December 2004, Sandra Snowden, a resident of Bay Harbor Islands, Florida, sued in federal court after town officials refused to let her erect her own Nativity scene next to a synagogue's Hanukkah menorah displayed alongside a causeway. Town leaders countered that the menorah, which commemorates the rededication of the Temple in Jerusalem after a Jewish military victory in 165 B.C., was a secular symbol of freedom. They offered to let Snowden install a Christmas tree rather than a Nativity scene. Ten days after Christmas day, Judge Cecilia Altonaga ordered the town to let Snowden put up her Nativity scene.

The National Christmas Tree Fiasco

Nobody knows exactly which Christmas tree is the official National Christmas tree in the United States. The National Park Service, the U.S. Forest Service, the National Christmas Tree Association, the U.S. Capitol, and the White House all have Christmas trees called the National Tree.

In 1923, First Lady Grace Coolidge gave permission for the District of Columbia Public Schools to put up a Christmas tree in President's Park (now known as the Ellipse), south of the White House. The organizers named the tree the National Christmas Tree. In 1973, President Richard M. Nixon responded to environmentalists and had a living tree planted on the Ellipse as the National Christmas Tree, to be tended by the National Park Service. Every year the president presses a button to light the tree as part of a major White House event.

Although the tree outside the White House is undoubtedly the most popular national Christmas tree, on April 28, 1926, President Calvin Coolidge desig-nated the General Grant Tree in Sequoia National Park in California as the Nation's Christmas Tree. The General Grant Tree is the third largest tree in the world. During a Christmas ceremony each year, park rangers place a large wreath at the base of the tree.

Another national Christmas tree stands in the Blue Room of the White House. Each year since 1966, members of the White House staff select the official White House Christmas Tree from trees grown by members of the National Christmas Tree Association. The White House Floral Department decorates the tree.

Meanwhile, every Christmas season since 1964, a beautifully decorated Christmas tree called the National Holiday Tree has stood on the West Front lawn of the United States Capitol. Since 1970, the tree has been cut from a national forest and supplied by the United States Department of Agriculture Forest Service.

So which tree is the official National Christmas Tree?

CHRISTMAS CRIMES and CATASTROPHES

STARTING CHRISTMAS OFF WITH A BANG

On Christmas Day in 1869, sixteen-year-old John Wesley Hardin went to the small Texas town of Towash in search of some holiday cheer and a good game of cards. A year earlier, Hardin had killed a former slave for threatening him with a stick, shot the three soldiers who tried to arrest him for the murder, and fled to Navarro County, where he found a job as a teacher in a one-room schoolhouse. While playing cards, Hardin apparently lost his Christmas spirit and got into a heated dispute with a man named James Bradley over a card hand. The men agreed to settle the argument in a showdown on a deserted Towash street, where Hardin shot Bradley dead. In 1878, Hardin, known to have murdered more than twenty men, was imprisoned. He emerged fourteen years later a changed man, abandoned his violent ways, and raised his three children in Gonzales, Texas. Three years later in a bar in El Paso, a gunslinger, eager to enhance his own fame, shot Hardin in the back.

390

Roman emperor Theodosius ordered the massacre of more than seven thousand inhabitants of the city of Thessalonica in Macedonia.

820

Byzantine emperor Leo V was murdered in a palace conspiracy.

1717

Floods ravaged the coast of Holland, killing thousands.

1912

At the age of twelve, Adlai Stevenson accidentally fired an old .22 rifle during a Christmas party at his home, killing one of the female guests.

1942

Admiral Dalans, murderer of Bosinier de la Chapelle, was sentenced to death.

1950

The Stone of Scone, a coronation stone stolen from Scotland by England's King Edward I in 1296, was stolen from Westminster Abbey and smuggled back to Scotland.

1951

Harry Tyson Moore, an NAACP official in Florida, was killed by a bomb.

1953

An avalanche of lava from New Zealand's Ruapehu volcano killed 150 people.

1954

Memphis blues pianist Johnny Ace, best known for his 1954 hit single "Pledging My Love," accidentally shot himself in the head at age twenty-five while playing Russian roulette on Christmas Eve.

1957

Serial killer Ed Gein was declared insane by a jury and sentenced to life imprisonment. The killers portrayed in the movies *Psycho* and *Silence of the Lambs* were reportedly based on Gein.

1964

A hurricane in the Indian Ocean killed four thousand people in Ceylon and three thousand people in the Indian province of Madras.

1971

The worst hotel fire in history killed 163 people at Taeyokale Hotel in Seoul, Korea.

1972

An earthquake hit Managua, Nicaragua, killing ten thousand people and destroying 75 percent of the buildings. Billionaire Howard Hughes was among the three thousand Americans in Managua when the two-and-a-half-hour series of quakes struck.

1974

Cyclone "Tracy" virtually destroyed Darwin, Australia.

1974

Marshall Fields crashed his car through a White House gate, stationed himself near the mansion with a suspicious load strapped to his back, and held off police for four hours. The load on his back contained emergency flares.

1976

The Egyptian ship SS *Patria* sank in the Red Sea, killing some one hundred Muslims returning from a pilgrimage.

1984

Vietnamese troops attacked Cambodian rebels, forcing 63,000 Cambodians to flee to Thailand.

Christmas Sleighing

On Christmas Day in 1996, six-year-old JonBenet Ramsey, the reigning Little Miss Colorado, was murdered in her home in Boulder. Her parents, John and Patsy Ramsey, called police at 5:52 the next morning to report that their daughter was missing. The Ramseys found a two-and-a-half-page ransom note demanding $118,000—the exact amount of money millionaire John Ramsey had received as a Christmas bonus as president of a high-tech company—in exchange for JonBenet. The note, written in felt-tip pen on paper torn from a legal pad, matched paper in the Ramsey home. The police and the FBI arrived at the Ramsey home, made only a cursory search, and set up phone-tapping equipment. By 7:30 a.m., John Ramsey had gathered the $118,000 ransom. The ransom note named a time by which the kidnapper would call, but the phone never rang.

A detective asked John Ramsey and his friend Fleet White, a wealthy oil executive, to search the house for anything unusual. Ramsey and White began in the basement. At 2 p.m., in a room where Patsy Ramsey had hidden some Christmas presents, John Ramsey found his daughter's dead body under a white blanket. She had been beaten, sexually assaulted, and strangled with a crude garrote—a cord wrapped around her neck, wrenched tighter and tighter as the killer twisted a foot-long stick attached to it. Duct tape covered her mouth and her hands were tied together with a cord.

Distraught, John Ramsey removed the duct tape from his daughter's mouth, carried the body and blanket upstairs, and placed her next to the family's Christmas tree, disrupting the crime scene and destroying crucial evidence.

With no signs of an intruder, suspicion fell on John and Patsy Ramsey. The investigation into JonBenet's murder continued for more than two years, and the Ramseys were brought to trial. In October 1999, a grand jury dismissed the case, which remains unsolved.

Mother and Child

On December 24, 2002, 27-year-old substitute teacher Laci Peterson, then seven months pregnant with a boy, mysteriously disappeared from her home in Modesto, California.

Laci's husband, Scott Peterson, told police that he had gone to the marina in Berkeley that morning to go fishing. He said his wife had planned to go food shopping and then walk their dog, Mackenzie, through nearby East La Loma Park. Peterson said Laci's SUV was parked in the driveway and her purse, containing her car keys, was hanging in the bedroom closet. Her uncharged cell phone was found in her vehicle.

A neighbor said she witnessed Scott loading an object wrapped in a large blue tarp into his truck that morning. Scott claimed that the tarp contained eight-foot umbrellas for work. Other witnesses said they saw Laci in the park with her dog at ten o'clock in the morning. Later that day, neighbors found the family dog, Mackenzie, running loose in the neighborhood, wearing a collar and muddy leash.

Law enforcement agencies conducted an extensive manhunt of East La Loma Park and surrounding areas, searching forests and waterways.

Police suspected Scott, but Laci's family came forward to support him. Scott did produce a receipt from the Berkeley marina stamped December 24 (but without any printed indication of the time). Scott maintained that he knew nothing about Laci's disappearance, refused to talk with the media, and showed up every morning to work at the volunteer command center set up by friends and family at a nearby hotel in the hopes of finding Laci.

Police unearthed photos of Scott posing with a woman named Amber Frey, with whom they suspected he was having a long-term affair. Police also discovered that Scott had taken out a $250,000 life insurance policy on Laci after he learned she was pregnant. Based on these findings, Laci's family ceased supporting Scott.

On April 13, 2003, police found the decomposed body of a newborn baby boy on the San Francisco Bayshore, north of Berkeley. The next day, one mile away from where the baby's body had been recovered, police found the decomposed and decapitated body of a woman. DNA tests confirmed that the bodies were Laci Peterson and her son, Conner.

Five days later, Police arrested Scott, who had dyed his hair blond and grown a beard, near the home of his parents in La Jolla, California, to prevent the possibility that he might flee across the nearby border to Mexico. At the time of his arrest, Scott was driving a car he had purchased using his mother's name, and was in possession of $15,000 in cash, four cell phones, camping equipment, Viagra, and his brother's driver's license.

On November 12, 2004, a jury in San Mateo Country convicted Scott for the murder of both Laci and their unborn son, and on March 16, 2005, the judge sentenced Scott to death.

1985

Intertribal fighting in South Africa claimed fifty-three lives.

1987

Police recaptured Lynette "Squeaky" Fromme, who had escaped from prison two days earlier. A follower of convicted murderer Charles Manson, Fromme was serving a life sentence for her attempt to assassinate President Gerald Ford on September 5, 1975.

1989

Ousted Rumanian dictator Nicolae Ceausescu and his wife Elena were executed by protestors with machine guns following a popular uprising.

1989

Billy Martin, manager of the New York Yankees, was killed in a car accident.

1997

Russian mountain climber Anatoli Boukreev was killed at age thirty-nine by an avalanche while attempting to ascend Annapurna, a 26,000-foot peak in Nepal.

2000

A fire at a Christmas party at the Dongdu Disco in Luoyang, China, killed more than three hundred people.

2003

Beagle 2, Britain's first unmanned Martian space probe, was scheduled to land on Mars on Christmas Day, but instead disappeared without a trace. Investigators could not pinpoint how the $90 million probe vanished. British scientists suspected that a Martian heat wave and accompanying dust storms thinned the atmosphere, causing Beagle 2 to enter the atmosphere too fast and crash, or the space probe's parachutes and the airbags simply failed to deploy properly.

Naughty or Nice?

El Niño, the extensive warming of the central and eastern Pacific Ocean every three to seven years, causes a period of fierce winds and rainfall across the Pacific. Peruvian fishermen named the phenomenon El Niño (literally, "the boy-child"), as a reference to the baby Jesus because its appearance usually coincides with Christmas. The name has nothing to do with El Niño's sometimes cataclysmic repercussions.

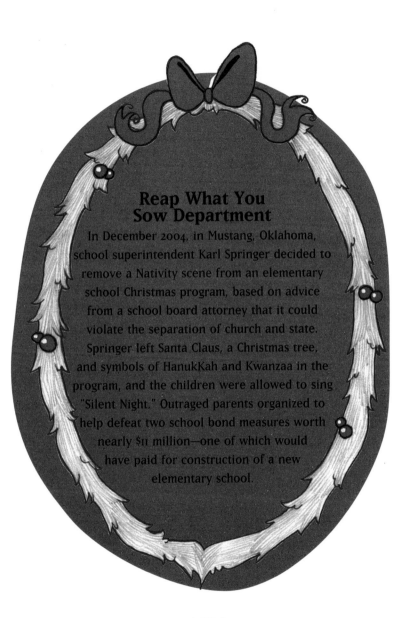

Reap What You Sow Department

In December 2004, in Mustang, Oklahoma, school superintendent Karl Springer decided to remove a Nativity scene from an elementary school Christmas program, based on advice from a school board attorney that it could violate the separation of church and state. Springer left Santa Claus, a Christmas tree, and symbols of Hanukkah and Kwanzaa in the program, and the children were allowed to sing "Silent Night." Outraged parents organized to help defeat two school bond measures worth nearly $11 million—one of which would have paid for construction of a new elementary school.

Santa's Sex Change

In 2000, the Kentucky Commission on Human Rights ruled that Wal-Mart did not did not discriminate against a woman by firing her from playing Santa Claus in the store. Five years earlier, Wal-Mart employee Marta Brown volunteered to play Santa Claus for the Wal-Mart store in Morganfield, Kentucky, wearing the traditional Santa costume. When a small girl asked her mother why Santa had breasts, the mother complained to Wal-Mart, and the store managers quickly replaced Brown with a male Santa. Brown quit her job and sued Wal-Mart for $67,000 in lost wages, pain, and suffering.

Wal-Mart argued that Brown did not make a convincing Santa, and the Kentucky Commission on Human Rights ruled that Wal-Mart had the right to replace Brown to avoid hurting Christmas sales and confusing children. "Unfortunately, Ms. Brown's debut as Santa Claus was less than successful," said Commissioner Karen McCord.

Wal-Mart company spokesman Mike Maher said the company stood by its decision to replace Brown based on her gender. "The bottom line is we do believe Santa Claus is a man," said Maher. "He has always been portrayed as a man."

Christmas Disease

Christmas Disease is a type of hemophilia, a hereditary disease in which the blood does not clot normally. Approximately 15 percent of all hemophiliacs have Christmas Disease, due to a lack of clotting factor number nine, also known as the Christmas factor. The disease is named after a ten-year-old boy named Stephen Christmas, one of the first patients to be treated for it. The disease has nothing to do with Ebenezer Scrooge or any allergic reactions to hearing the same Christmas songs played repeatedly in department stores.

Naked Christmas

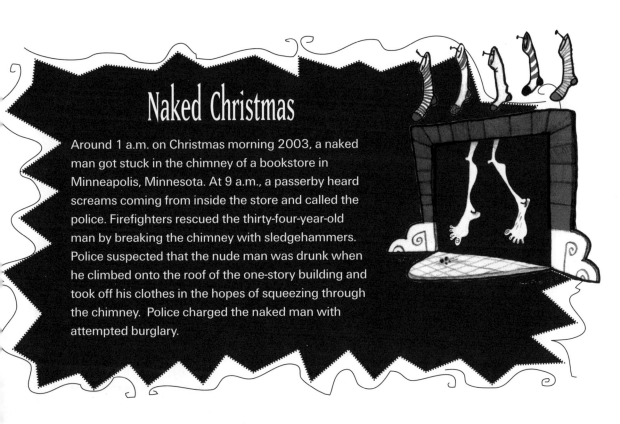

Around 1 a.m. on Christmas morning 2003, a naked man got stuck in the chimney of a bookstore in Minneapolis, Minnesota. At 9 a.m., a passerby heard screams coming from inside the store and called the police. Firefighters rescued the thirty-four-year-old man by breaking the chimney with sledgehammers. Police suspected that the nude man was drunk when he climbed onto the roof of the one-story building and took off his clothes in the hopes of squeezing through the chimney. Police charged the naked man with attempted burglary.

Santa's Sex-Discrimination Suit

In November 2000, Donna Underwood of Mount Hope, West Virginia, filed a sex discrimination lawsuit against SantaPlus of St. Peters, Missouri, which hired her to play Santa Claus at the Crossroads Mall in Beckley. The company fired her after one day on the job when a mall manager complained about having a female Santa.

"The mall said they couldn't have a female Santa," Underwood said. "They said, 'mythically, Santa was a man'."

Underwood had decided to apply for the Santa job because a year earlier, while working at a T-shirt shop in the mall, she played the part of Santa for one day when the man hired to play Santa in the mall failed to show up for work. She enjoyed bringing happiness to the children and seeing their faces light up with joy.

Underwood insisted that she could play Santa as well as any man. She claimed that when she wore the Santa suit, the white beard and wig, no one could tell she was a woman.

She even lowered her voice and was the ideal weight of a typical Santa.

After firing Underwood, SantaPlus rehired her to work as an elf at the mall's Santa display, but after a few days she quit, unable to derive any spiritual fulfillment from the job. That's when she decided to file the sex discrimination suit. SantaPlus offered Underwood $3,000 to drop the lawsuit, but she refused.

Two weeks later, Underwood was back at work at the Crossroads Mall, this time as Mrs. Claus, a role that paid the same salary as Santa. "I still think it's discrimination," she said, refusing to drop the lawsuit, which sought reinstatement, back pay, and unspecified damages.

CHRISTMAS BASH

On December 24, 1994, the Christmas Twins, 31-year-old sisters Lorraine and Levinia Christmas, crashed head-on as they headed to each other's homes in Flitcham, England, to deliver Christmas presents. The Christmas Twins suffered chest injuries, whiplash, and concussions. "We did a double take when we first received details of the accident," a police spokesman told the Reuters news service. "We thought it was a practical joke."

CROAKED ON CHRISTMAS

795
Adrian I
Pope (772–795)

1530
Babar
*Turkish prince who founded
the Mogul Empire in India*

Civilly Disobedient Santas

On December 2, 2001, after city officials of Kensington, Maryland, banned Santa Claus from attending a Christmas tree-lighting ceremony, dozens of defiant white-bearded, red-suited Santas roared into town in pickup trucks and motorcycles in a brazen act of Christmas civil disobedience, receiving cheers from the townspeople.

1683
Kara Mustafa Pasa
Grand vizier of the Ottoman Empire who was beheaded by order of the sultan; his head was brought to the sultan on a silver dish

1761
Elisabeth Petrovna
Russian empress who staged a coup d'état against a baby— the infant emperor Ivan VI

1926
Yoshihito
123rd emperor of Japan

1927
Sergei Sazonov
Russian Foreign minister (1910–1916)

1940
Agnes Ayres
*Silent-screen actress who played
Rudolf Valentino's paramour
in* The Sheik *and* The Son
of the Sheik

1954
Liberty Hyde Bailey
*American botanist and
horticulturist*

1946
W. C. Fields
*Comedian who insisted that he
hated children and Christmas*

1977
Charlie Chaplin,
*the actor, writer, and director
who starred in* The Tramp, The Kid,
The Gold Rush, City Lights, *and*
Modern Times, *and co-founder
of United Artists Chaplin once
said he was more widely known
than Jesus. Several months after
his death, his body mysteriously
disappeared from the village
cemetery in Vevey, Switzerland.
It was never found.*

DEADLY CHRISTMAS

More Americans die from natural causes on Christmas than on any other day of the year, according to a 2004 study by sociologists at the University of California–San Diego and Tufts University in Boston.

On Christmas, 12.4 percent more Americans die from heart attacks and other natural causes than usual. The researchers did not count deaths from suicide, murder, or accidents, but factored in the general tendency for deaths due to natural causes to peak during the winter.

Death rates probably increase over the holidays because people feel too busy or too festive to seek immediate medical attention. Also, changes in hospital medical staffs during the holidays may compromise the quality of medical care. A 2004 study by Duke University Medical Center researchers revealed that heart attack patients admitted to hospitals during the winter holidays are more likely to die than those admitted during the rest of the year.

1979
Lee Bowman
Actor who starred in the television detective drama The Adventures of Ellery Queen

1979
Joan Blondell
Actress who appeared in more than eighty films, most notably A Tree Grows in Brooklyn *and* The Blue Veil, *and starred as Lottie Hatfield on the television series* Here Come the Brides

1980
Karl Doenitz
German admiral and Adolf Hitler's hand-picked successor who was tried for war crimes in Nuremberg and sentenced to ten years in prison

1994
Zail Singh
President of India (1982-1987)

1995
Dean Martin
Singer and actor who teamed with Jerry Lewis to become one of the most phenomenal successes in show business history. He was a member of Frank Sinatra's famous "Rat Pack," starred in the Matt Helm movies, and host of a television variety series, The Dean Martin Show

1983
Joan Miro
Spanish surrealist painter

1996
Rupert John
Governor General of the Grenadines (1970-1976)

1997
Denver Pyle
Actor who played Uncle Jesse Duke on the television series The Dukes of Hazzard

Acknowledgments

I am gratefully indebted to my editor, Laura Ross, for championing my cause, sharing the visions of sugar plums that dance in her head, and laughing all way; my publisher, J.P. Leventhal, for pushing me to decorate the tree with as many ornaments as possible; my agent, Jeremy Solomon, for keeping the Yule log burning bright; and Terry Adams for guiding my sleigh by suggesting the idea in the first place. I am also grateful to Lisa Weber for her stunning illustrations that make this book so merry and bright; Sheila Hart for masterminding the cover, the interior design, and for making sure the stockings were hung by the chimney with care; my copyeditor Sara Cameron for making a list and checking it twice; photo researcher Jennifer Thompson Stone for finding pictures of mommy kissing Santa Claus; and Wendy Vierow for helping me deck the halls with boughs of folly. Above all, thanks to Debbie for being my true love, and to Ashley and Julia for being my two turtle doves.

Bibliography

"A Christmas Carol: Dickens' Gift to the Movies" by Susan Wloszczyna, *USA Today*, December 15, 1992

After Jesus: The Triumph of Christianity (Pleasantville, New York: Reader's Digest, 1992)

"All that Glitters Is in Pinecrest," by Elinor J. Brecher, *Miami Herald*, December 19, 2002

"An Astronomical Re-Appraisal of the Star of Bethlehem" by David Clark, John Parkinson, and Richard Stephenson, *Quarterly Journal of the Royal Astronomical Society*, December 18, 1977, p. 443

"An Earth-friendly Christmas Tree: Company Rents Out Real Trees in Pots-Roots and All" by Rick Bowmer, Associated Press, December 24, 2004

"Argentine Policemen Try to Arrest a Greenpeace Activist Dressed Up as Santa Claus Outside the Argentine Congress" by Marcos Brindicci, Reuters, December 17, 2004

"At Santa U., Classmates Learn the Ins and Outs of Work as St. Nick" by James Temple, *The Kenesaw State University Sentinel*, November 17, 2004

"Aztec Idols, Yes; Mary and Jesus, No?" by Linda Chavez, *USA Today*, December 7, 1994

"Babies Among Carolers Making a Joyful Noise" [ED: Pls. confirm this change.OK]by Edna Gundersen, *USA Today*, December 4, 1998

"Ban Santa? Here's Coal in Your Stocking" by Alcestis "Cooky" Oberg, USATODAY.com, December 22, 2004

Biblical Literacy by Rabbi Joseph Telushkin (New York: Morrow, 1997)

The Book of Jewish Knowledge by Nathan Ausubel (New York: Crown, 1964)

"Canadian NORAD Region Names Santa Claus Escort Pilots," Canadian Department of National Defence, December 16, 2002

"Cardiac Mortality Is Higher Around Christmas and New Year's Than at Any Other Time," by David P. Phillips, Jason R. Jarvinen, Ian S. Abramson, and Rosalie R. Phillips, *Circulation*, December 21, 2004

"Census Bureau Facts for Features #15: The Holiday Season" (Washington, D.C.: U.S. Census Bureau's Public Information Office, December 6, 2000)

"Christmas Comes to Cuba" by Robert A. Sirico, *The New York Times*, December 19, 1997

Christmas Customs and Traditions: Their History and Significance by Clement C. Hattes (Dover, 1976)

Christmas Customs Around the World by Herbert Wernecke (Westminster Press, 1979)

"Christmas Gifts Cursed with Bad Luck," *Wireless Flash Weird News*, December 16, 2004

"Christmas Pickles, and Flying Kangaroos: Amusing Holiday Hints to Add Sparkle to Your Season" by Joyanne Pursaga, *The Manitoban*, February 20, 2002

"Christians Protest Actions That Play Down Christmas' Religious Nature," by Richard Willing, *USA Today*, December 21, 2004

"Christmas Sex Dangers Revealed," BBC News Online, December 23, 1999

"Christmas Twins Have True Seasonal Bash," Reuters News Service, December 26, 1994

"Cuba: Silent Nights," by Scott Wilson, Washington Post Foreign Service, December 24, 2000

"Epidemiology of Reindeer Parasites" by Odd Halvorsen (*Parasitology Today*, December 1986, pp. 334-339)

The Film Encyclopedia by Ephraim Katz (New York: Perigee, 1979)

Familiar Quotations, Fifteenth Edition by John Bartlett, edited by Emily Morison Beck (New York: Little, Brown, 1980)

"Getting Rowdy—All for a Good Claus" by Marc Ramirez, *Seattle Union Record*, December 3, 2000

The Guinness Book of Records, edited by Peter Matthews (New York: Bantam, 1993)

The Harvard Biographical Dictionary of Music, edited by Don Michael Randel (Cambridge, Massachusetts: the Belknap Press of Harvard University Press, 1996)

"Holiday Cheer Masks Wartime Fear; 'I'll Never Forget This Christmas'" by Laurence Jolidon, *USA Today*, December 26, 1990

Holiday Lights!: Brilliant Displays to Inspire Your Christmas Celebration by David Seidman (North Adams, Massachusetts: Storey Publishing, 2003)

"Holiday Thoughts," USATODAY.com, December 23, 2004

"In-Santa-ty in San Jose" by Joyce Slaton, *Wired News*, December 7, 1998

"Instilling the Santa Spirit" by Elizabeth Johnson, *American Profile*, December 19-25, 2004

The Jerusalem Bible (New York: Doubleday, 1966)

Jesus: A Life by A.N. Wilson (New York: W.W. Norton, 1992)

Jesus: The Evidence by Ian Wilson (New York: HarperCollins, 1996)

Jewish Literacy by Rabbi Joseph Telushkin (New York: Morrow, 1991)

The Jews of America by Frances Butwin (New York: Behrman House, 1973)

"Judge Refuses to Let 'Grinch' Steal Christmas" by Al Andry, *Cincinatti Enquirer*, December 7, 1999

Knickerbocker's History of New York by Washington Irving (New York: G. P Putnam, 1865)

Laugh with Hugh Troy: World's Greatest Practical Joker by Con Troy (Wyomissing, Pennsylvania: Trojan Books, 1983)

"Lighting Up for Nostalgic Christmas" by Debbie Howlett, *USA Today*, December 19, 1989

"Love or Hate It, Landfill Dominates" by Tom O'Neill, *The Cincinnati Enquirer*, March 18, 2003

"Live Christmas Tree Rentals Woo Environmentalists," CBC News, December 24, 2004

"Mall Requires Real Beards for Santa Claus" by Meagan Hamby, San Joaquin Delta College *Impact*, December 6, 2002

"Mall Santa Claus Throws Fit Over Crying Baby" by Hilary E. MacGregor, *Los Angeles Times*, December 24, 1999

"Museum Showcases Tackiness" by Burton Cole, *Tribune Chronicle*, July 30, 2002

Mythology by Edith Hamilton (New York: New American Library, 1940)

National Climatic Data Center weather records

National Lampoon Songbook, edited by Sean Kelly (New York: Cherry Lane Music, Inc., 1976)

"Nativity Sets from Largest Collections in the U.S. Can Be Seen in D.C., on the Web and at Their Home at UD's Marian Library," University of Dayton Press Release, November 26, 2002

"Naughty Santa" by Bruce Weir, *Avenue*, December 2004

"Naughty Santas Subvert Christmas Spirit" by Janelle Brown, *Wired Magazine*, December 18, 1997

"National News Release," New Zealand Police, December 19, 2004

"Nicks at Night" by Bill Werde, *Time Out* [ED: What city? New York], December 6-13, 2001

"NORAD tracking Santa Claus Christmas Eve" Press Release (Colorado Springs: North American Aeorspace Defense Command, December 24, 1997)

"NY Santas Rescue Bicyclist," Associated Press, December 20, 1994

1001 Christmas Facts and Fancies by Alfred C. Hattes (A.T. De La Mare, 1954)

"Operation Santa Claus" by Tim Harper, *Sky* magazine, December 1997

Oshkosh B'Gosh Annual Report, 1996

"Our Constitutional Christmas" by James J. Kilpatrick, *Wilmington Morning Star*, April 23, 2001

Panati's Extraordinary Origins of Everyday Things by Charles Panati (New York: Perennial, 1987)

The Pentateuch and Haftorahs, Second Edition edited by Dr. J. H. Hertz (London: Soncino Press, 1968)

The Physics of Christmas: From the Aerodynamics of Reindeer to the Thermodynamics of Turkey by Roger Highfield (New York: Little, Brown, 1998)

"Poll: Fake Christmas Trees Grow Popular" by Gary Langer, ABC News, December 23, 2004

"Record Santa Plans Hot Up," BBC News, June 8, 2004

"Santa Claus a Drunk Perv?" by William Burrill (*Toronto Star*, December 13, 2000)

"Santa Olympics Kick Off" by Brian Bernbaum, CBS/AP, November 4, 2004

"Santa Rampage 1999" by Rico Gagliano, *LA Weekly*, December 24 - 30, 1999

"Santarchy" by Summer Burkes, *San Francisco Bay Guardian*, December 27, 2000

"Santarchy 1999! Rebels with a Claus" by Steve Moramarco, *Whoa!*, December 20, 1999

"Santas Run for Record" by Gemma Collins, News.Scotsman.com, December 5, 2004

"School for Santas" by Bill Geist, CBS, December 15, 2002

"Sexy Singapore Santas Hand Out Thousands of Condoms," Associated Press, December 22, 2003

"Snoopy's Success Was Christmas Miracle" by Bill Keveney, *USA Today*, December 11, 2000

"Social Distortion" by Rob Hill, *Bikini Magazine*, June-July 1998

"Sterling Wal-Mart Resells Donated Toys," Associated Press, December 5, 2002

Strange Stories, Amazing Facts by the Editors of Reader's Digest (Pleasantville, New York: Reader's Digest, 1976)

Television Comedy Series by Joel Eisner and David Krisnsky (Jefferson, North Carolina: McFarland, 1984)

"That Snapshot with Santa Will Cost You," Associated Press, December 18, 2000

"The Lights Before Christmas" by Sheila Anne Feeney, *New York Daily News*, November 29, 1998

"The Odd Truth" compiled by Joey Arak, CBSNEWS.com, December 23, 2004

"The Santafication of McMurdo" by Allison Barden, *The Antarctic Sun*, January 2, 2005

"The Working Life: Job as Shopping-mall Santa Is Cyclical, But Recession-proof" by Jim McKay, *Pittsburgh Post-Gazette*, November 26, 2002

"'Tis the season for Tree Farmers," by Chris Foreman, *Pittsburgh Tribune-Review*, December 20, 2004

"U.S. Supreme Court Dismisses Effort to Abolish Christmas Holiday," Reuters News Service, April 19, 2001

"A Visit from St. Nicholas" by Clement C. Moore (*Troy Sentinel*, December 23, 1823)

"Volunteer Santa Claus Molested Neighborhood Children," by James L. Eng, Associated Press, October 21, 1997

"Wal-Mart Had Right to Stop Female Santa," by Chris Poynter, *Louisville Courier-Journal*, October 10, 2000

www.christopherradko.com/

www.foxnews.com/etcetera/121100/santa_suit.sml

"Woman Sues Over not Being Santa," Associated Press, December 19, 2000

Wonderful Copenhagen: The Official Tourism Site of Copenhagen and the Surrounding Area (www.woko.dk)

The World Book Encyclopedia (Chicago: World Book, 1985)

World Religions: From Ancient History to the Present, edited by Geoffrey Parrinder (New York: Facts on File, 1971)

"Yes, Virginia, There Is a Santa Claus" by Francis P. Church, *The New York Sun*, 1897

"You Better Watch Out!," by Ylan Q. Mui, *Washington Post*, December 15, 2002

Index

About the Author

Joey Green—author of *Polish Your Furniture with Panty Hose, Paint Your House with Powdered Milk, Wash Your Hair with Whipped Cream,* and *Clean Your Clothes with Cheez Whiz*—got Jay Leno to shave with Jif peanut butter on *The Tonight Show*, Rosie O'Donnell to mousse her hair with Jell-O on *The Rosie O'Donnell Show*, and Katie Couric to drop her diamond engagement ring in a glass of Efferdent on *Today*. He gave Meredith Vieira a facial with Elmer's Glue-All on *The View*, conditioned Conan O'Brien's hair with Miller High Life beer on *Late Night with Conan O'Brien*, and rubbed French's Mustard on Wayne Brady's chest on *The Wayne Brady Show*. He has been seen polishing furniture with Spam on *NBC Dateline*, cleaning a toilet with Coca-Cola in *The New York Times*, and washing his hair with Reddi-wip in *People*.

Green, a former contributing editor to *National Lampoon* and a former advertising copywriter at J. Walter Thompson, is the author of more than thirty books, including *The Zen of Oz: Ten Spiritual Lessons from Over the Rainbow, You Know You've Reached Middle Age If...,* and *The Mad Scientist Handbook*. A native of Miami, Florida, and a graduate of Cornell University, he wrote television commercials for Burger King and Walt Disney World and won a Clio Award for a print ad he created for Eastman Kodak. He backpacked around the world for two years on his honeymoon, and lives in Los Angeles with his wife, Debbie, and their two daughters, Ashley and Julia.